Tasty treats from your Snackmaker

R&R PUBLICATIONS MARKETING PTY LTD

Sunbeam

Sunbeam has been manufacturing small appliances since 1921, and has since built its reputation on an unwavering commitment to the highest quality manufacturing standards.

Throughout our history, we have been responsible for some of the most innovative products to hit the Australian market. As a result, appliances such as the Sunbeam Mixmaster™, Pop-Up Toaster and the Electric Frypan have become Australian icons.

Sunbeam's continual innovation of the humble small appliance, has seen the brand maintain its market leadership for generations.

The commitment from the Sunbeam design team to transform the basic snackmaker, has been recognised by design and industry awards. The simple toasted snack has come a long way from the traditional cheese jaffle to gourmet-toasted meals.

There is something about the taste of melted cheese on toasted bread. It has become a staple snack food for many Australians, made popular many years ago by the old campfire 'jaffle iron'.

Cooking a jaffle was as simple as buttering two pieces of bread, placing your favourite ingredients in the middle and holding the jaffle iron over the fire. The edges were sealed, bread golden brown with a delicious piping hot filling.

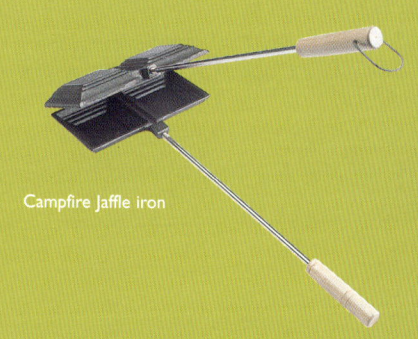

Campfire Jaffle iron

This style of snack was made increasingly popular in the mid-70s when the first electric jaffle maker was launched for domestic use. Sunbeam launched its first sandwich maker in 1977. Variations on the jaffle maker soon evolved with the sandwich maker and the sandwich grill. Today, snackmakers can be found in the majority of Australian homes.

A common complaint with the early snackmaker was the difficulty of cleaning. There were too many crevices and areas to trap food, especially melted cheese and breadcrumbs.

Identifying this, Sunbeam revolutionised the snackmaker with their EasyClean™ design. This design focused on eliminating dirt traps and integrating the wiring into the hinge to create a simple 'wipe-down' finish. This new EasyClean™ system was recognised with Sunbeam receiving an Australian DesignMark.

EasyClean™ Sandwich Maker

As Australian lifestyles changed through the 90s to embrace 'café-style' dining, so too did the snackmaker. The new millennium saw the birth of the domestic sandwich press. The principles of which were taken from the commercial sandwich press found in delis and cafes to create gourmet snacks on Turkish or focaccia bread. Café-style snacks can now be enjoyed at home.

Sunbeam has two sandwich presses, the Café Press™ and the Café Grill, with flat and grill plates respectively. This style of snackmaker has become increasingly popular and now accounts for over half of the total number of snackmakers sold.

Café Press™

Sunbeam want to ensure that you get the most out of your snackmaker so we have come together with Master Foods of Australia and Dairy Farmers to demonstrate to you the limitless capabilities of snackmakers.

Happy toasting.

contents

INTRODUCTION	4-5
TYPES OF SNACKMAKERS	6-7
RECIPES	8
SIMPLE TOASTED SANDWICHES	8-9
SANDWICH GRILL RECIPES	10
GOURMET TOASTED SANDWICHES	10-18
SAVOURY PLATTER	20
PIZZAS AND MELTS	23-27
SANDWICH PRESS RECIPES	28
GOURMET SANDWICHES AND FOCACCIAS	28-43
PIZZA'S AND MELTS	44-48
ENTERTAINING IDEAS	51-55
JAFFLE MAKER RECIPES	56
JAFFLE SNACKS	56-59
PIES	61-66
SWEETS	68-72
SANDWICH MAKER RECIPES	74
FILLING COMBINATIONS	76-79
ENTERTAINERS	80-84
SWEET TREATS	87-88
FLAVOURED SPREADS	91
MASTERFOODS AND COON PRODUCTS	92-95
INDEX	96

INTRODUCTION

YOU CAN USE THE SANDWICH GRILL AND SANDWICH PRESS TO COOK SANDWICH FILLINGS, ELIMINATING THE NEED TO USE OTHER APPLIANCES.

With the busy life styles of today, sandwiches and snacks take on an increasing role in our daily eating pattern. We are all familiar with the after school snack, late night study supper, a quick meal before rushing to a club meeting or the Saturday night easy dinner. When creating the recipes, we restricted the use of other appliances and cooking utensils to a minimum. The versatility of the snackmakers is demonstrated by their ability to successfully produce toasted sandwiches as well as pizzas and melts and to chargrill ingredients needed for café style gourmet treats. A platter of savouries for a crowd or a sweet treat for afternoon tea can also be enjoyed.

E Argyriou

Grilled Vegetables
Grilled vegetables are the "new ingredient" in sandwiches. No need to buy them ready-cooked, they are easy to cook in the Sandwich Grill or Sandwich Press.

Grilled Eggplant
1. Wash the eggplant and cut into 4mm thick slices, either lengthwise or crosswise.
2. Pre-heat the Sandwich Grill or Sandwich Press. Spray the base plate with oil spray, place on the slices, spray the tops and close the lid. Cook for 2-3 minutes or until soft and cooked.
Note: The hinged Sandwich Grill may take longer. Turn the slices over after 2 minutes if needed.
3. Remove to a plate, use immediately or place in a covered container and add an oil and vinegar dressing. Refrigerate.

Grilled Sweet Potato, Carrots, Zucchini
1. Wash and peel the sweet potato and carrots, wash the zucchini.
2. Cut into 3mm thick slices lengthwise or diagonal, making sure they are an even thickness.
3. Cook as per eggplant for 2 minutes or to your liking. Use immediately or refrigerate.

Grilled Capsicums
1. Cut a slice off the top and base of the capsicum then cut down the 4 sides, cutting 4 flat pieces. Trim off the inner membranes.
2. Pre-heat the Sandwich Grill or Press and spray the base plate with oil. Place on the capsicums, skin side up, spray the tops and close the lid. Cook for 3 minutes until blistered. Remove the capsicums and place in a plastic bag, closing the bag to retain the steam; stand for 20 minutes.
Note: You may need to turn the slices if using the Sandwich Grill.
3. Skin the capsicums by sliding a small sharp pointed knife under the skin, then pulling the skin off. Use immediately or store as per eggplant.

Grilled Onions
1. Peel the onions and cut into 2mm thick round slices.
2. Cook as per eggplant.

Caramelised Onions
1. Peel and slice the onions into 3mm thick round slices.
2. Place a sheet of baking paper on the base plate. Place on the onion slices, spray with oil and cover with a second sheet of baking paper and close the lid. Cook for 1 minute. Open the lid and lift the paper and sprinkle the onions with 2 to 3 teaspoons of white or brown sugar. Re-cover and close the lid. Cook for 1 to 2 minutes. Stir onions around every 30 seconds.

Grilled Orange, Lemon and Lime Slices (for sandwich garnishes)
1. Sprinkle slices lightly with sugar. Place between 2 sheets of baking paper in the pre-heated Sandwich Grill or Press.
2. Cook for 2 minutes or until desired colour is achieved.

Grilling Steaks
1. Pound the meat out very thinly with a meat mallet. Season as desired and brush both sides with a little oil. Place in the pre-heated Sandwich Grill or Press, close the lid and cook for 2 to 3 minutes, or until done.
2. When done, proceed to assemble and cook the sandwich. Meats suitable include minute steak, rump steak, veal or pork schnitzel.

Grilled Chicken
Chicken tenderloins: flatten slightly. Chicken breast fillets: small fillets may be pounded to desired thinness; large fillets may be sliced thinly with a sharp knife.
Cook as for steaks, check after 1 1/2 minutes and cook a little longer if necessary, until cooked through.

Thin Sausages
Place in the preheated Sandwich Grill or Press. Cook for 3 to 4 minutes. Turn occasionally.

Cheese Tips for Toasted Sandwiches
Melting the cheese to the right degree of creamy smoothness is essential for the enjoyment of your toasted sandwich, melts or quick pizza.
For a good result, follow the tips below.

1. The cheese will melt to a smoother consistency if it is at room temperature. Remove the portion to be used from the refrigerator 20 minutes before it is used.
2. Cook the sandwich for 2 to 3 minutes depending on thickness of the cheese or until the cheese melts to a soft consistency. With the Sandwich Grill and Press, it is so easy to take a look during the cooking stage. Overcooking will cause the separation of the fat in the cheese which results in the cheese becoming stringy and tough.
3. The cheese stated in the recipes may be changed to one of your preferred choice.
4. Cheese melts and quick pizzas are very easy to make in the Sandwich Grill and Press. Slices of block cheese, ready sliced cheese or shredded cheese may be used. Have the cheese at room temperature, arrange over the melts or pizza and cover with a piece of baking paper. Close the lid and support it with your hand, so it just touches the surface of the cheese without flattening the ingredients. Hold in place until cheese melts. Check regularly until the cheese melts to the desired consistency. Peel the paper off while hot.
5. When using thicker slices of cheese cut from a block do not cover the bread to the edge, leave a 1/2cm perimeter. The cheese will melt and come to the edge of the crust and will not spill out.
6. Remember, cold cheese straight from the refrigerator will take longer to melt than cheese at room temperature.

Cutting tips
Cutting hot toasted sandwiches needs special attention so as not to dismantle, the fillings.

1. Cut with the point of a large sharp knife held at a 75° angle, using a hopping backward movement as you cut. If the length of the knife blade is placed down on the sandwich, the pressure exerted to cut the sandwich will push out the filling.
2. An electric knife cuts a hot sandwich with ease and does not disturb the filling. Place the blade along the sandwich and press to start button. It will cut through with ease.

You can choose from quick and simple combinations of fillings or more elaborate gourmet fillings.

DIFFERENT
SNACK

Sandwich Press

▲ *Recommended breads for the Sandwich Press:*
Turkish or focaccia bread, and bagels. Also great for wrap-style snacks using lavish or Lebanese bread.
Recommended fillings for the Sandwich Press:
Chicken breast-fillet or roast beef, salmon or tuna, sun-dried tomatoes, swiss cheese and roasted vegetables.

Create your own gourmet-toasted snacks at home with a Café-style Sandwich Press. The Sandwich Press is a four-slice snackmaker with two separate cooking plates held together by hinged arms on the side. The essence of this café-style floating hinge design is that it adjusts to toast any size snack, from high sandwich stacks to tasty bagels. You can choose from two types of Sandwich Presses, one which has flat cooking plates top and bottom, the other comes with ribbed plates (top and bottom) to create snacks with authentic grill marks.

Sandwich Grill

▲ *Recommended breads for the Sandwich Grill:*
High-top loaves, Turkish bread, Focaccia, standard and super-size breads of all varieties.
Recommended fillings for the Sandwich Grill:
Leg ham or salami, tasty cheese and tomato, with your favourite mustard or spread.

The Sandwich Grill available in both two and four-slice, features ribbed cooking plates on the top and bottom. The lid is hinged but has the ability to elevate to a degree. You should choose a Sandwich Grill that features a floating hinge and a variable locking latch at the front as this will give you greater flexibility with the size of your toasted snacks. Allowing you to toast the thickest sandwiches and focaccia's.

Delicious toasted snacks and quick meals can be created in any one of Sunbeam's Snackmakers.

MAKERS AVAILABLE

Sandwich Maker

The Sandwich Maker is similar to a Jaffle Maker in that the edges are sealed during toasting enclosing the filling. What differentiates it is that a sandwich maker will also cut and seal the sandwich diagonally into triangles, creating two snacks to enjoy. The Sandwich Maker available in both two and four-slice is great for weekend lunches and when entertaining as it creates more snacks to share.

▲ *Recommended breads for the Sandwich Maker:*
Standard and super-size bread: white, wholemeal, multigrain, rye, sourdough or any other variety.
Recommended fillings for the Sandwich Maker:
Turkey and cheese with cranberry sauce, ham and cheese or leftover mincemeat. Also suitable for moist fillings such as baked beans, spaghetti and cream corn.

Jaffle Maker

The Jaffle Maker is a two-slice snackmaker, which toasts your snack by clamping down firmly on the two pieces of bread to seal the edges only, creating a large pocket. Jaffle makers will hold a substantial amount of filling creating a hearty snack or quick meal, ideal for hungry teenagers. A good Jaffle Maker will create a complete seal around the edge of the bread to hold in all the fillings.

▲ *Recommended breads for the Jaffle Maker*
Standard and super-size breads: white, wholemeal or multigrain. You can also use both Puff and Shortcrust pastry for sweet snacks.
Recommended fillings for the Jaffle Maker
The simple, delicious cheese jaffle, but also particularly suitable for moist fillings such as baked beans, spaghetti and creamed corn or create a sweet treat using apples and cinnamon.

THE SANDWICH GRILL

Introduction

*Quick and simple combinations of fillings or more elaborate and generous fillings. When teamed with a variety of breads, wonderful toasted sandwich snacks and quick meals can be made in the **Sandwich Grill**. The lid is hinged, but has the ability to elevate to a degree, allowing thick sandwiches and focaccia to be made.*

SIMPLE TOASTED SANDWICHES

Sandwich combinations of 2 or 3 ingredients using sliced sandwich bread, or the thicker cut toast bread which gives a higher sandwich. White, wholemeal, soy linseed, wholegrain or rye bread may be used. Quantities are for 2 sandwiches which can be doubled for a 4 sandwich maker.

Method of Making – for all simple toasted sandwiches. Spread the sandwich bread lightly with softened butter or margarine. Spread any spreadable filling on unbuttered side and top with remaining ingredients listed. Close the sandwich with the buttered side facing up.

Preheat the **Sandwich Grill**. When green light turns on, place the sandwiches onto the grill plate and close the lid. Cook for 2 to 3 minutes. Remove to cutting board and cut in half. Allow to cool a little before eating as some fillings retain heat and can burn if eaten immediately. Refer to pages 4 and 5 for assembly and cutting tips.

For low fat sandwiches, spray lightly with canola or olive oil spray in place of spreading with butter or margarine.

FILLINGS FOR 2 SANDWICHES

Ham and Cheese:
2 teaspoons MasterFoods American Mustard
2 slices sandwich ham
2 COON Tasty Natural Cheese Slices

Ham, Tomato and Cheese:
Add slices of tomato to above combination

Cheese and Chutney:
2 tablespoons MasterFoods Country Harvest Fruit Chutney
4 x 4mm thick slices COON Extra Tasty Natural Cheese cut from the end of the block

Pizza Style:
2 tablespoons MasterFoods Tomato and Chilli Pickle
6 thin slices Italian salami
4 tablespoons Mil Lel Shredded Mozzarella Cheese, OR,
2 COON Light and Tasty Natural Cheese Slices

Parmesan Chicken:
2 tablespoons MasterFoods Chunky Salsa
2 or 3 slices cooked chicken breast
2 tablespoons Mil Lel Shredded Parmesan Cheese

Cheese and Gherkin:
2 tablespoons MasterFoods Gherkin Relish
4 x 4mm slices Cracker Barrel Extra Sharp Vintage Cheddar Cheese cut from the end of the block

Ham and Relish:
2 tablespoons MasterFoods Tomato Relish
100g shaved ham
2 Fred Walker Swiss Cheese Slices

Simple toasted sandwiches

Egg and Honey Mustard:
3 hard boiled eggs, chopped and mixed with
2 teaspoons MasterFoods Honey Wholegrain Mustard and
1 tablespoon mayonnaise

Fruit Loaf and Cheese:
4 slices sultana loaf or spiced fruit bread
4 x 4mm slices COON Smooth and Mild Natural Cheese, cut from the end of the block

Carrot and Sultana:
Mix together: 2 tablespoons sultanas
4 tablespoons COON Light and Tasty Natural Shredded Cheese, and 4 tablespoons grated carrot

The above simple toasted sandwiches may also be made in a floating hinge snackmaker, such as the Sandwich Press (with flat or ribbed plates).

GOURMET TOASTED SANDWICHES

Toasted sandwiches with generous and interesting fillings. A variety of breads are featured which can be interchangeable. Some cooked ingredients, eg. grilled capsicum and eggplant, are used in the fillings. These may be purchased already prepared, cooked on a grill or cooked in the Sandwich Grill. Refer to pages 4 and 5 for the method of how to grill using the Sandwich Grill.

Vegetable and Cheese Sandwich

INGREDIENTS

4 slices grilled sweet potato

1 medium onion, caramelised

6 snow peas, washed, dried and strings removed

4 x 4mm slices Cracker Barrel Extra Sharp Vintage Cheddar Cheese cut from the end of the block

4 toast (thicker) bread slices, buttered

METHOD

1. Prepare the sweet potato and caramelised onion (see pages 4 and 5).
2. Place grilled sweet potato on unbuttered side of bread, top with the onion, snow peas and cheese. Close the sandwiches with the remaining bread slices, buttered side up.
3. Place in preheated **Sandwich Grill** and cook for 3 minutes.

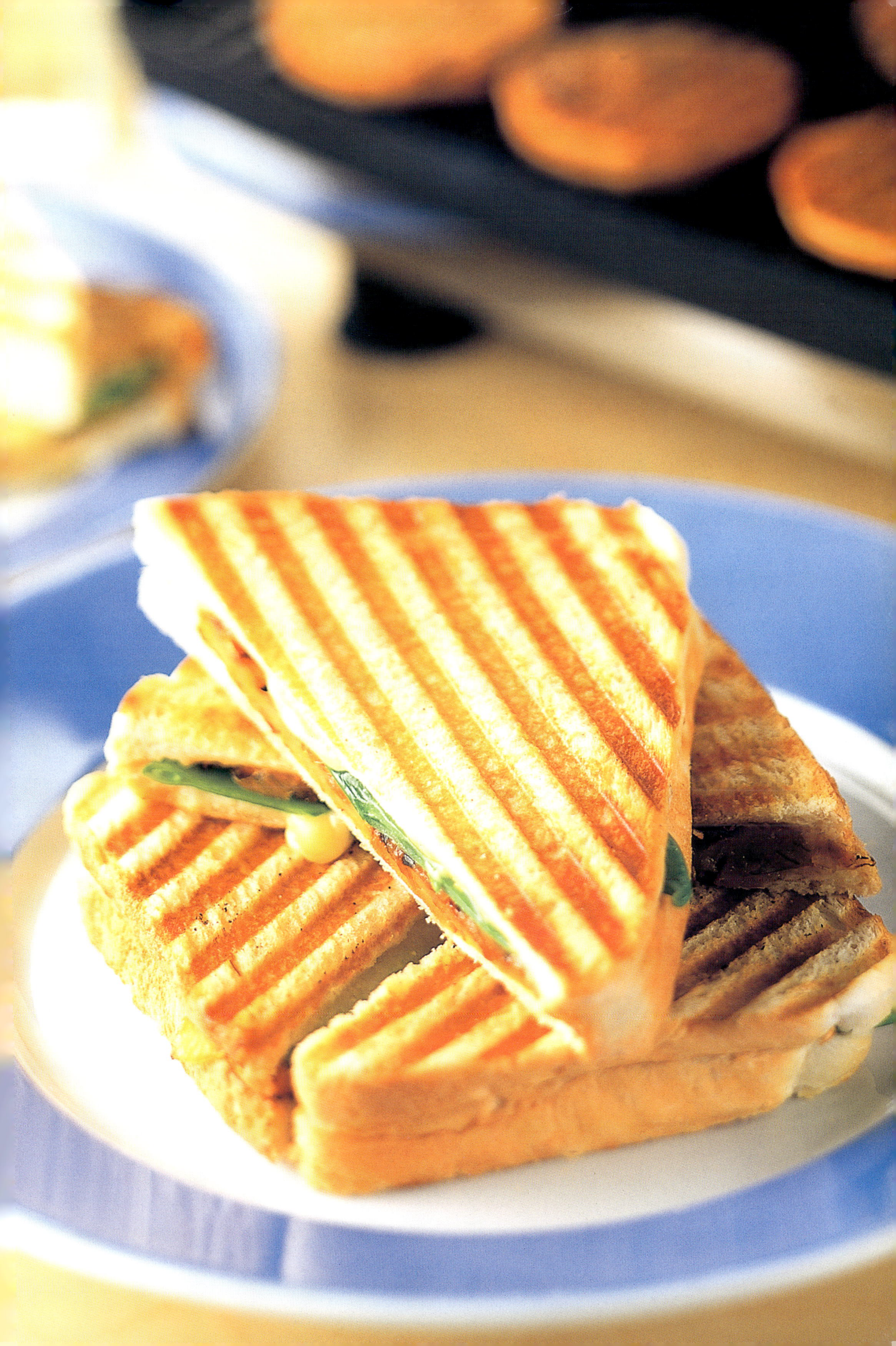

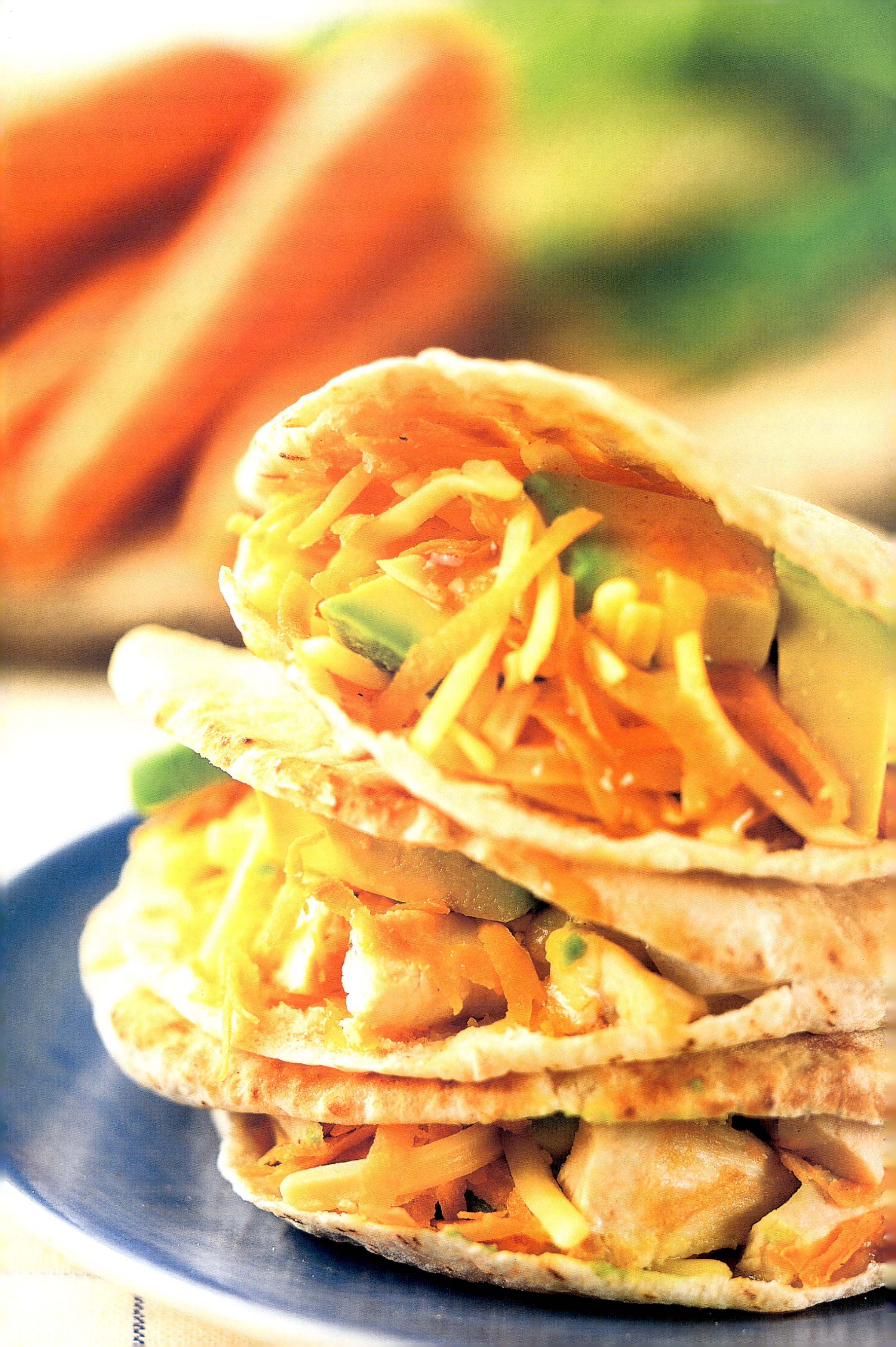

GOURMET TOASTED SANDWICHES

Chicken and Avocado Pocket Bread

INGREDIENTS

2 pita pocket breads

2 tablespoons hummus

½ cup diced cooked chicken

½ ripe avocado, mashed

½ cup grated carrot

½ cup COON Tasty Natural Shredded Cheese

salt and MasterFoods Ground Black Peppercorns, to taste

MasterFoods Sweet Chilli Sauce

METHOD

1. Split the pocket breads enough to open the pocket. Spread each, on one side of inside with hummus.

2. Mix chicken, avocado, carrot and cheese together. Season to taste with salt and pepper. Divide and spread into each pocket bread. Squirt in the Chilli Sauce.

3. Place in the pre-heated **Sandwich Grill** and cook for 2 to 3 minutes.

GOURMET TOASTED SANDWICHES

Bacon and Egg Buns

INGREDIENTS

2 large hamburger buns

2 teaspoons MasterFoods Tomato Sauce

1 rash bacon, cooked and diced

2 small eggs

MasterFoods Garlic and Herb Salt

METHOD

1. With a sharp pointed knife, slanting inwards, cut a circle 1cm in from the edge, on top of each bun. Lift out the bread circle and pull out enough soft bread to make a deeper hole.

2. Place a teaspoon of tomato sauce into each hole, place in the bacon pieces and break an egg into each. Season and replace the top, resting lightly. Place into the pre-heated **Sandwich Grill** and cook for 5 minutes. Do not clip the latch, allow the lid to rest on the buns.

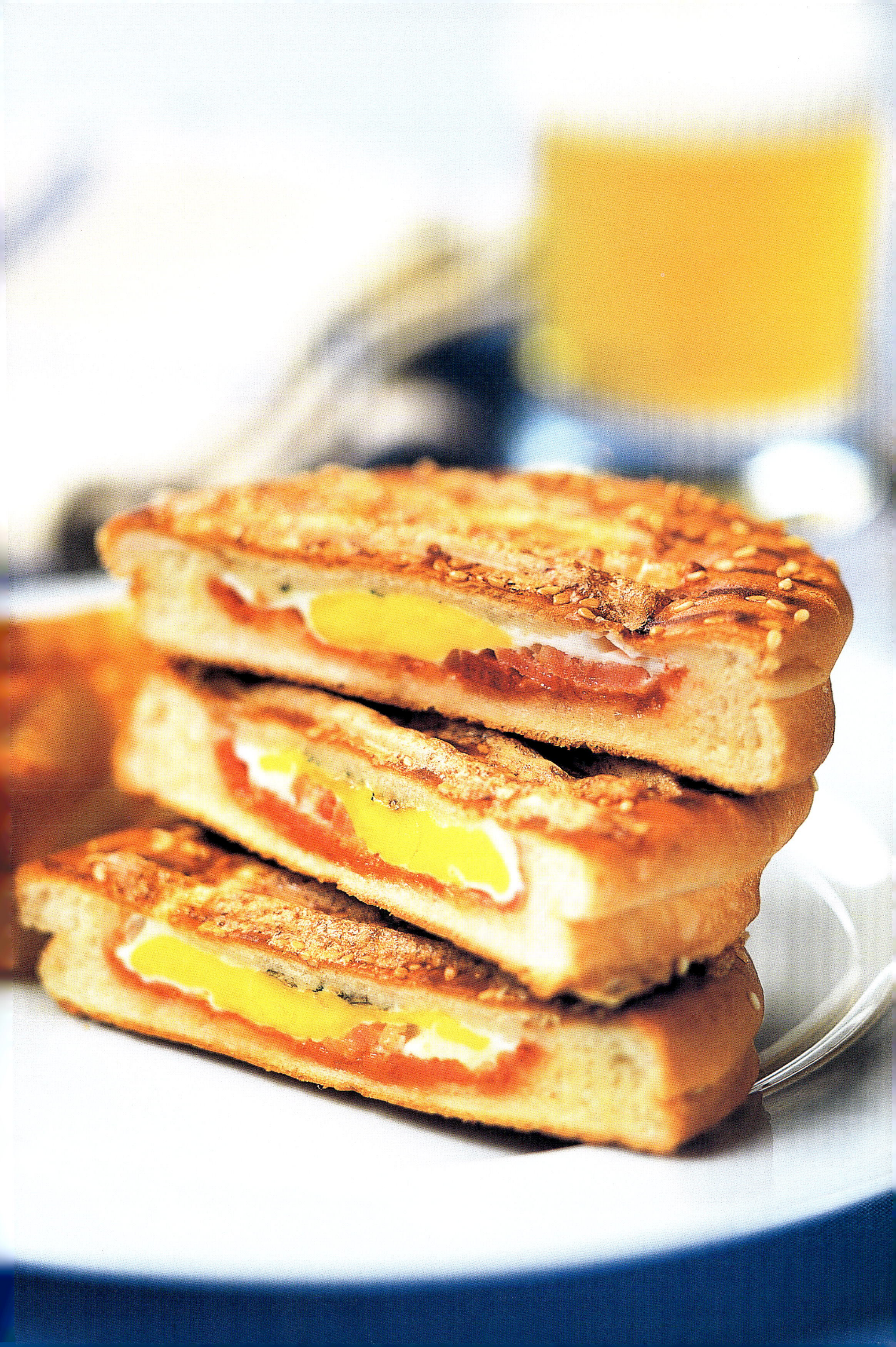

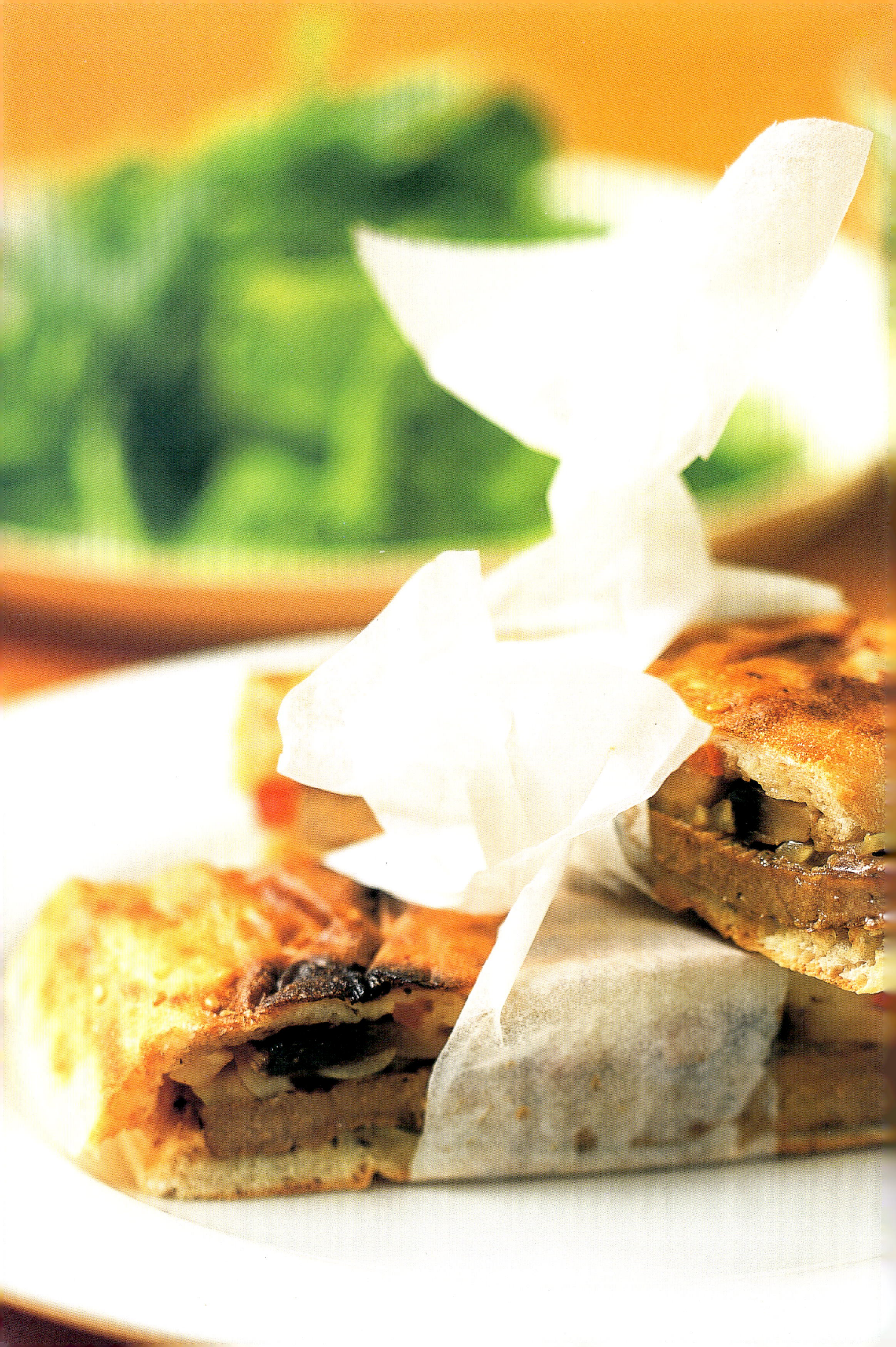

GOURMET TOASTED SANDWICHES

Steak Sandwich Deluxe

INGREDIENTS

2 slices minute steak, pan fried

MasterFoods Italian Herbs (sprinkled on steak)

1 small onion, thinly sliced

MasterFoods Steak or Barbeque Sauce

2 large mushrooms, sliced

½ red capsicum, cut into thin strips

½ of a long loaf Turkish Pide

METHOD

1. Cut the ½ pide into 2 pieces and split through the centre. (Freeze the remainder for future use).

2. Assemble the prepared ingredients in order listed onto the base, close with the top piece.

3. Place in the preheated **Sandwich Grill** and cook for 2 minutes. Serve hot with salad garnish.

> **Note:** The steaks can be cooked in the **Sandwich Grill**. Refer to pages 4 and 5 for instructions. Rump or Fillet steak may be used. Pound out very thinly with a meat mallet.

GOURMET TOASTED SANDWICHES

Muffin Break

INGREDIENTS

4 English muffins, split

200g shaved ham

4 slices canned pineapple

4 COON Tasty Natural Cheese Slices

canola oil spray

METHOD

1. Divide the ham and place on bottom half of each muffin. Top with pineapple slice, cheese slice and close with muffin top.

2. Pre-heat the **Sandwich Grill,** when green light is on, open lid and quickly spray base plate with a light spray of canola oil. Place on the muffins and quickly spray the tops. Close lid and cook for 2 to 3 minutes or until the cheese has melted sufficiently.

Serves 4

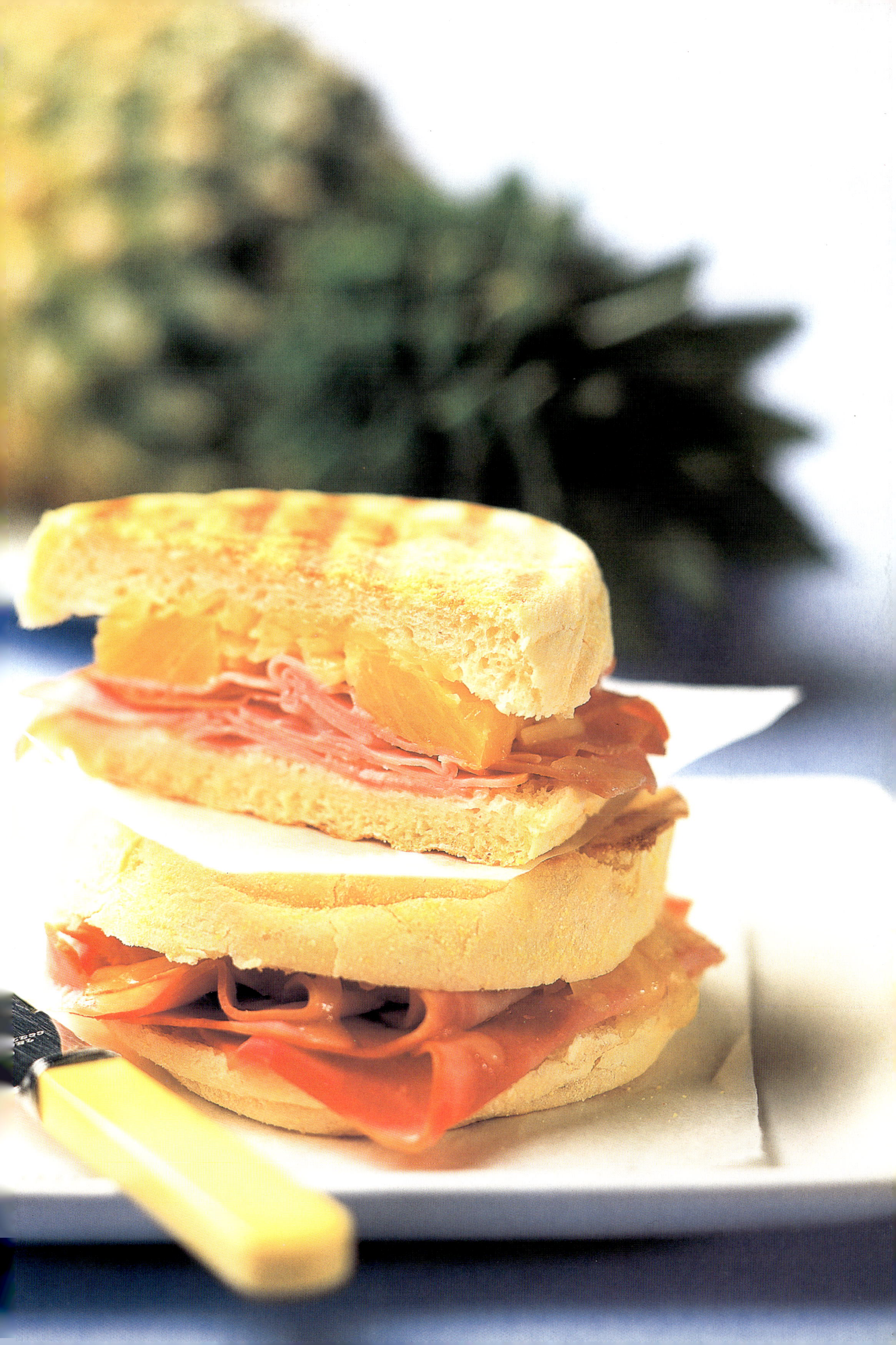

SAVOURY PLATTER

A platter of cocktail savouries ca
with the crouton base made in th

Savoury Platter

CROUTON BASE (for 12 savouries)

INGREDIENTS

3 slices super size sliced bread

canola or olive oil spray

METHOD

1. Cut 4 rounds from each bread slice with a 4cm scone cutter.

2. Preheat the **Sandwich Grill**. Spray the base plate with oil and arrange the bread bases on the plate in 3 rows. Spray the tops, close the lid and cook for 2 minutes or until medium golden in colour.

Remove and top with desired topping.

TOPPINGS

Pesto and Semi-dried Tomato

Spread each crouton with MasterFoods Freshly Blended Basil and top with semi-dried tomato.

Turkey and Relish

Spread each crouton with MasterFoods Tomato Relish, top with a pile of shaved turkey and sprinkle lightly with MasterFoods Poppy Seeds.

Honey, Mustard and Ham

Spread each crouton with MasterFoods Honey Wholegrain Mustard and top with shaved ham.

Blue Vein Relish

Spread each crouton with MasterFoods Gherkin Relish and top with crumbed Fred Walker Blue Vein Cheese.

Cocktail Sandwich

6 slices sultana bread or spicy fruit loaf, buttered

100g Fred Walker Blue Vein Cheese

METHOD

1. Spread blue vein cheese on unbuttered side of bread, close sandwich with buttered side up.

2. Cook in pre-heated **Sandwich Grill** for almost 2 minutes.

be quickly prepared
andwich Grill.

**Quick pizzas and a variety of melt
Tips for melting cheese topping ar**

Grilled Capsicum and Artichoke Pizza

PIZZAS AND MELTS

can be made in the **Sandwich Grill**.
given on page 5.

Grilled Capsicum and Artichoke Pizza

INGREDIENTS

2 Turkish pide buns, split

4 tablespoons MasterFoods Chunky Salsa

1 large onion, sliced and grilled

4 pieces grilled red capsicum

1 can Artichoke Hearts, quartered

12 seeded black olives

1½ cups COON Tasty Natural Shredded Cheese

1 sheet baking paper

METHOD

1. Spread each pide half with Salsa. Divide remaining ingredients between the pide halves, placing cheese on last.

2. Pre-heat the **Sandwich Grill.** Place the pizzas on the base plate and leave with lid open for 1 minute to heat the pide base.

3. Place a sheet of baking paper over the 4 pizzas and close the lid. Cook for 30 to 40 seconds or until cheese melts sufficiently.

4. Remove paper, easing backwards. Serve immediately.

Note: To grill onion and capsicum refer to pages 4 and 5.

Quick and Simple Pizza

INGREDIENTS

4 small size pita pocket breads

MasterFoods Tomato Sauce

3 slices sandwich ham, cut into strips

3 small tomatoes, sliced

½ cup Mil Lel Shredded Mozzarella Cheese

1 sheet baking paper

METHOD

1. Pre-heat the **Sandwich Grill** and place in the 4 pita bread. Cook for 1 minute to heat through.

2. Lift lid, squeeze tomato sauce onto each pita, quickly cover with ham strips, tomato slices and mozzarella cheese.

3. Place a sheet of baking paper on top of the pizzas, close the lid and cook until the cheese melts sufficiently, about 1 minute. Peel off the paper. Serve immediately.

PIZZAS AND MELTS

Ham and Mushroom Melts

INGREDIENTS

4 slices toast bread, buttered on one side

MasterFoods Tomato Mustard, twist and squeeze bottle

100g shaved ham, or 4 sandwich ham slices

2 large mushrooms, sliced

canola oil spray

4 COON Light and Tasty Natural Cheese Slices

1 sheet baking paper

METHOD

1. Assemble ingredients and pre-heat the **Sandwich Grill**. Place bread, buttered side down onto the base plate. Squeeze a zig-zag of mustard onto each slice, place on the ham and top with mushroom slices. Spray the mushrooms lightly with oil spray, close the lid and cook for 1 minute.

2. Open lid, place cheese slices on top of mushrooms, cover with the baking paper. Close lid and cook for 10 seconds or until cheese melts. Peel off paper. Serve immediately.

Serve 4

Note: COON Shredded Cheese or slices cut from your favourite block cheese may also be used. Close lid and cook for 10 to 20 seconds or until the cheese has melted sufficiently.

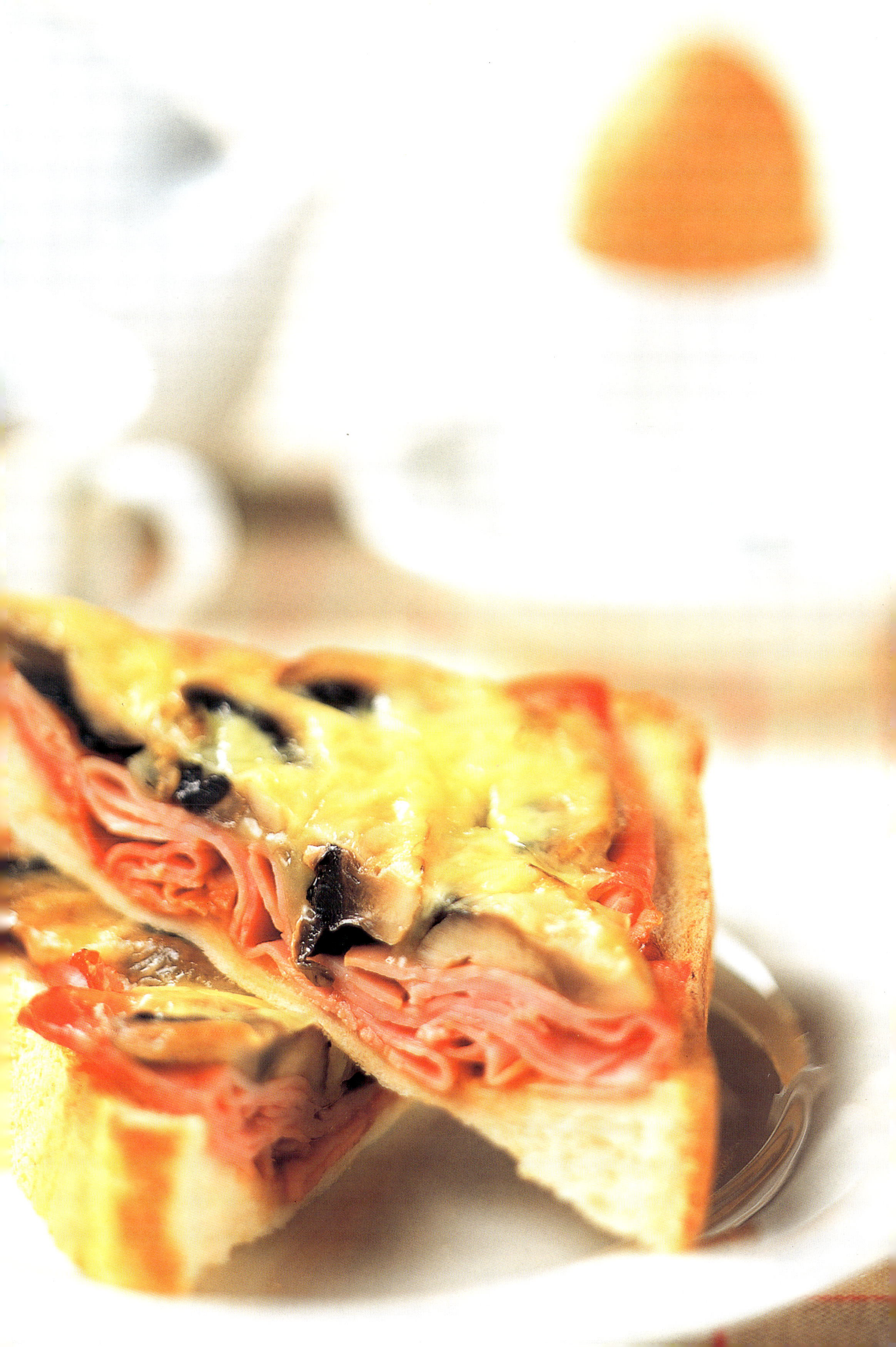

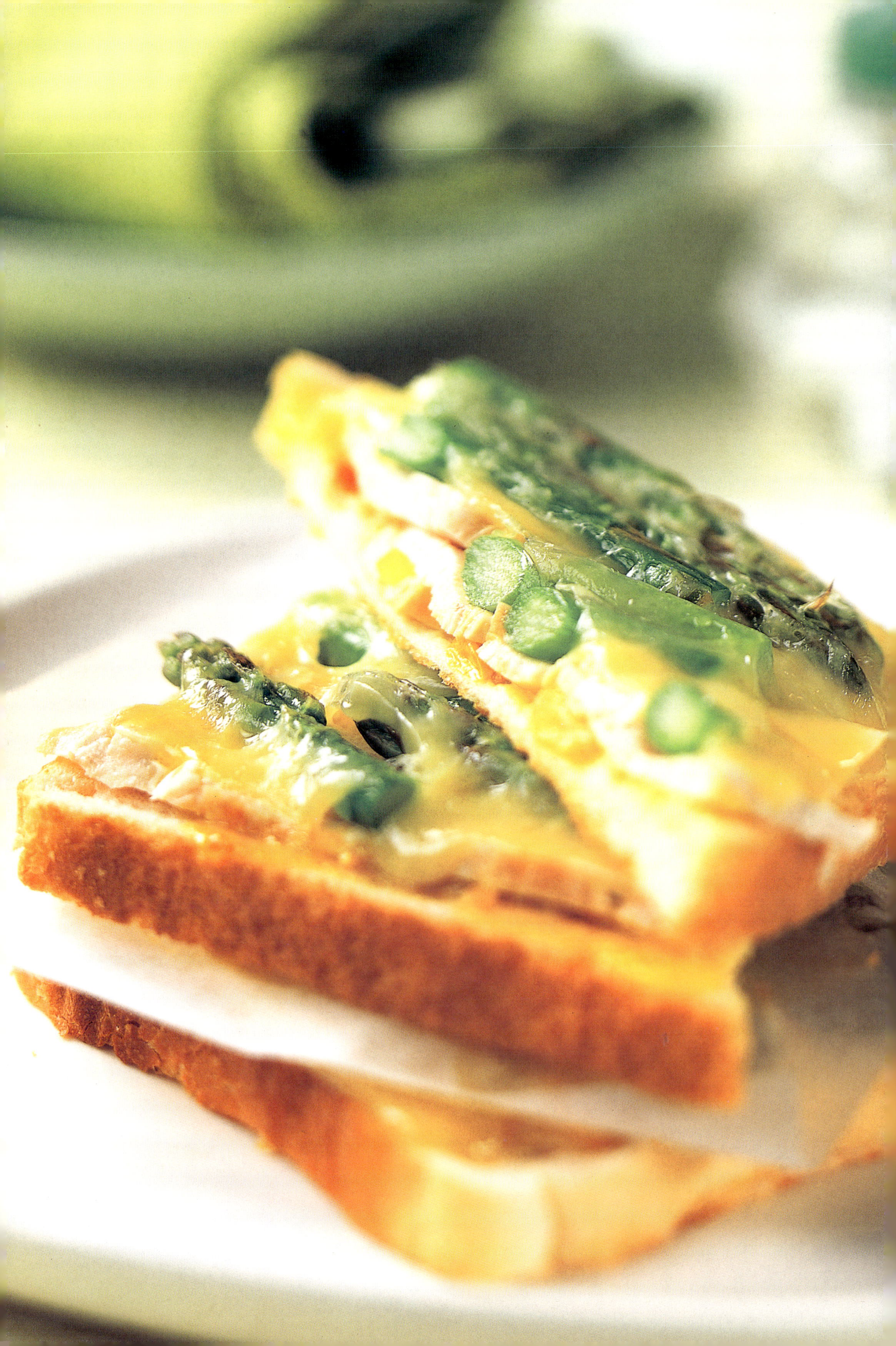

PIZZAS AND MELTS

Corn, Chicken and Asparagus Melts

INGREDIENTS

4 slices sandwich bread, buttered

2 tablespoons MasterFoods Corn Relish

1 cup cooked shredded chicken

1 can asparagus spears or cuts

4 slices COON Tasty Natural Cheese Slices

1 sheet baking paper

METHOD

1. Pre-heat the **Sandwich Grill**. Spread the corn relish on unbuttered side of bread. Place on the base plate of the **Sandwich Grill**, leaving the lid up, for 1 minute to toast the underside.

2. Arrange the chicken onto each slice, top with asparagus and cheese. Place the baking paper over the top, close the lid and cook for 10 to 20 seconds until cheese melts. Remove paper, serve immediately.

Note: Recipes in this section may also be made in the Sandwich Press, with the floating hinge.

THE SANDWICH PRESS

A variety of café style toasted snacks and sandwiches may now be made at home with the **Sandwich Press.** The floating hinge design adjusts to toast simple sandwiches, or high sandwich stacks using a variety of breads and buns. Recipes in this section may be made with the flat plate **Sandwich Press** or the ribbed plate **Sandwich Press.** The difference is only in the final appearance of the sandwich.

GOURMET SANDWICHES AND FOCACCIA

A selection of sandwiches with interesting and generous fillings, substantial enough for a meal. For quick and simple sandwiches refer to pages 4 and 5. When using sliced sandwich bread, choose the thicker cut toast bread or super sized sandwich bread for best results.

Chicken and Guacamole

INGREDIENTS

4 tablespoons MasterFoods Guacomole Style Dip

8 slices toast bread, buttered

½ of a barbeque chicken

salt and MasterFoods Cracked Black Peppercorns

80g Mil Lel Parmesan Cheese, shaved

METHOD

1. Shred the chicken meat, discarding skin and bones.

2. Spread the unbuttered side of 4 slices of bread with guacamole dip and arrange a generous portion of chicken on each side. Season with salt and pepper. Cover generously with Parmesan cheese shavings and cover each with remaining bread, buttered side up.

3. Place in pre-heated **Sandwich Press** and cook for 2 minutes or until golden.

> *Tip:* Shave the Parmesan from the end of the block with a potato peeler.

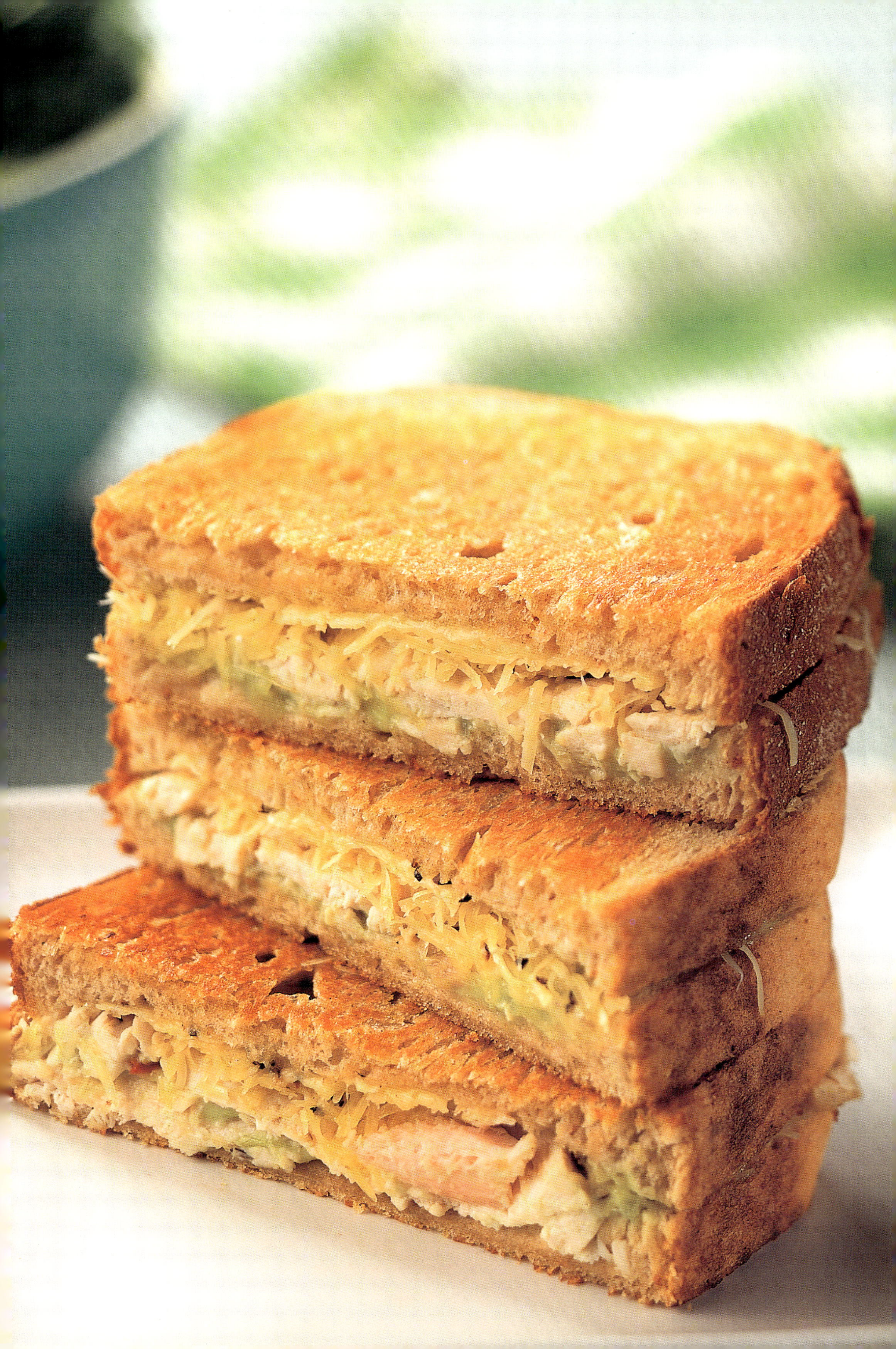

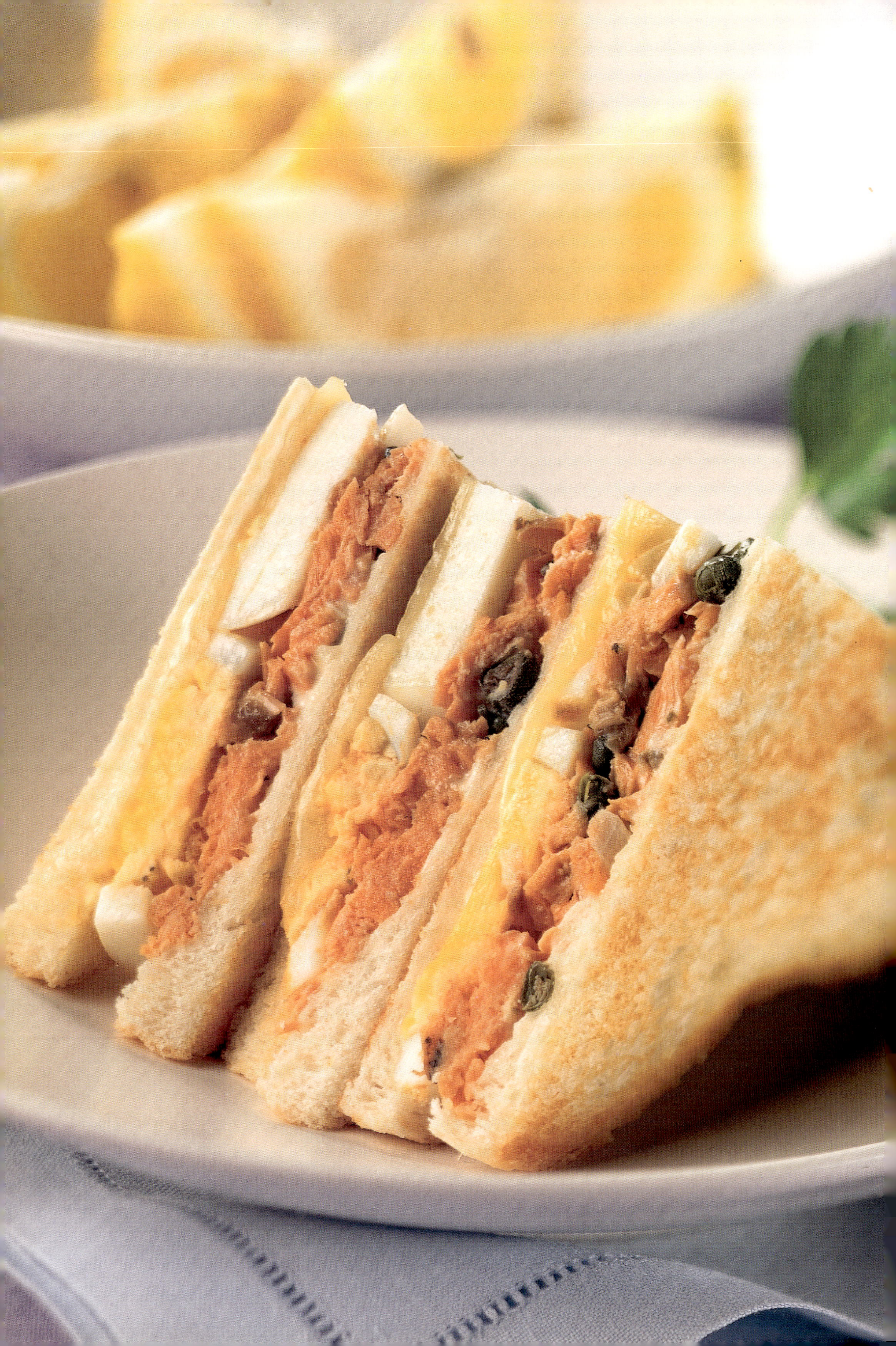

GOURMET SANDWICHES AND FOCACCIA

Salmon with Lemon Tartare

INGREDIENTS

220g can red salmon, drained

1 tablespoon baby capers, drained

2 tablespoons MasterFoods Lemon Tartare

4 slices super sandwich bread, buttered

2 hard boiled eggs, sliced

2 Fred Walker Swiss Cheese Slices

METHOD

1. Mix drained salmon, capers and lemon tartare together. Spread thickly onto unbuttered side of 2 bread slices. Arrange egg slices over the salmon and top with cheese slices. Close sandwich with remaining bread, butter side up.

2. Place into pre-heated **Sandwich Press** and cook for 3 minutes.

GOURMET SANDWICHES AND FOCACCIA

Sausage Sizzle on sourdough

INGREDIENTS

canola oil spray

4 thin pork sausages

1 large onion, sliced into rings

4 thick slices sourdough bread

MasterFoods Barbeque Sauce

4 x 3mm slices Cracker Barrel Extra Sharp Vintage Cheddar Cheese, cut from the end of the block

2 medium tomatoes, sliced

salt and MasterFoods Ground Black Peppercorns to taste

METHOD

1. Pre-heat the **Sandwich Press** and spray the base plate lightly with oil spray. Place on the sausages, spray lightly and close the lid. Cook for 3 minutes, open lid and half turn the sausages. Close lid and cook 3 minutes more or until cooked. Remove to a plate. Place the onion rings on the base plate, spray with oil and cook 2 minutes with lid closed. Remove.

2. Lightly spray the base plate with oil and place on 2 slices of bread. Squirt a zig-zag of barbeque sauce over each and place on the sausages, cut to fit. Cover with onion, cheese and tomato slices. Season with salt and pepper. Add extra sauce if desired. Cover with remaining bread slices and lightly spray tops with oil. Bring lid down in horizontal position and cook 3 minutes or until golden.

Note: Always keep the lid horizontal when toasting to ensure your fillings do not spill.

Variation: Spread bread with MasterFoods Mustard Pickle or Tomato Chutney in place of sauce.

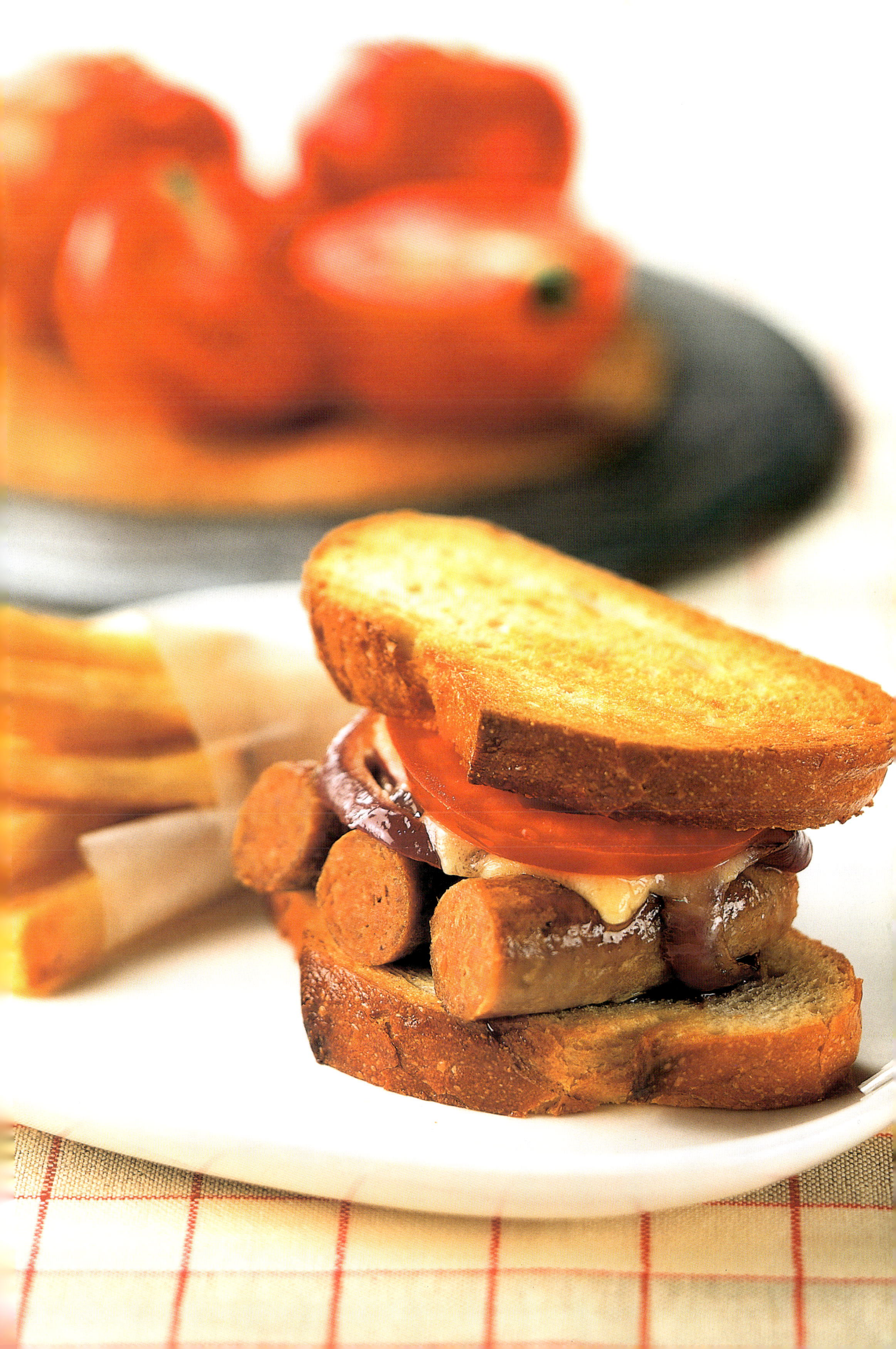

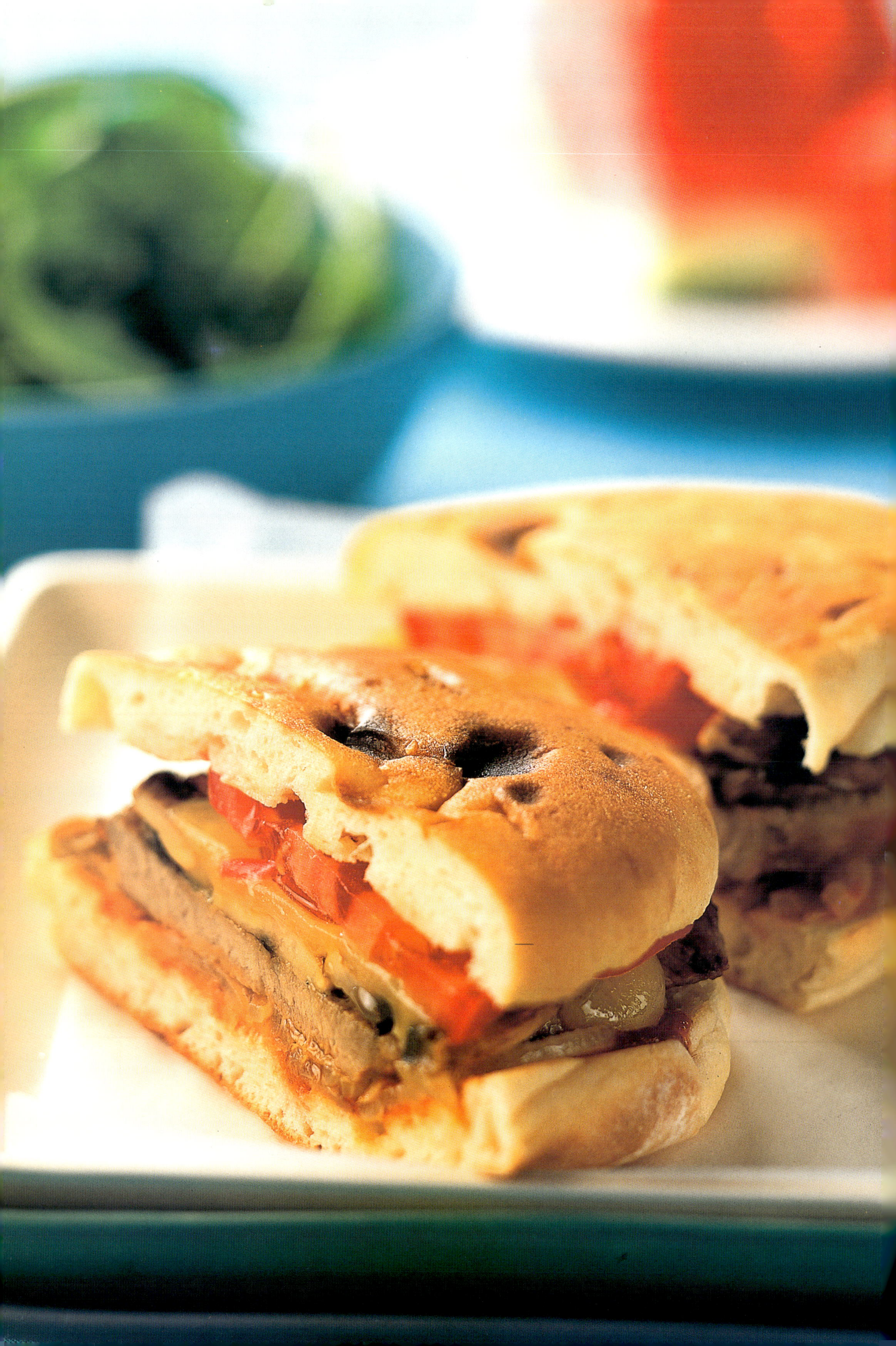

GOURMET SANDWICHES AND FOCACCIA

Steak and Mushroom Stack on Pide Bun

INGREDIENTS

2 minute steaks

MasterFoods Garlic and Herb Salt

canola or olive oil spray

2 large mushrooms, sliced

1 large onion, sliced into rings

2 oval Turkish pide buns, split through centre

MasterFoods Tomato Mustard

4 x 4mm slices COON Smooth and Mild Natural Cheese, cut from the end of the block

2 medium tomatoes, sliced

METHOD

1. Pound out the minute steak a little thinner with a meat mallet and season with Garlic and Herb Salt, set aside.

2. Pre-heat the **Sandwich Press** and spray the base plate lightly with oil spray. Place on the mushroom and onion slices, spray lightly on top and close the lid. Cook for 2 minutes, remove. Re-spray top and bottom plates, place on the minute steaks, close the lid and cook for 2 to 4 minutes or until cooked. Remove and keep warm.

3. Place bottom half of buns on the base plate, squirt on a zig-zag of tomato mustard and top each with the steak. Cover with onion and mushroom, top with cheese and tomato slices in given order. Cover with the top half of pide bun, close lid and cook for approximately 3 minutes or until cheese melts. Serve with a rocket salad garnish.

Variations: MasterFoods Tomato Sauce or Steak Sauce may be used in place of Tomato Mustard.

GOURMET SANDWICHES AND FOCACCIA

Chicken Salad and Cheese Lavash Roll

INGREDIENTS

Ingredients for 1 roll:

1 lavash sheet

2 tablespoons hummus

½ cup chopped cooked chicken, or

50g shaved chicken or turkey

½ cup grated carrot

salt and pepper to taste

½ cup COON Tasty Natural Shredded Cheese

1 sheet baking paper

½ cup shredded lettuce

MasterFoods Sweet Chilli Sauce

METHOD

1. Spread the lavash sheet with hummus. Sprinkle the chicken on the left half of the sheet and the carrot on the right half. Season to taste with salt and pepper if desired. Sprinkle the cheese over the entire surface.

2. Pre-heat the **Sandwich Press**, place the lavash sheet onto the base plate and cover with the baking paper. Close the lid and cook for 30 to 40 seconds or until cheese melts. Remove from press to a flat surface. Peel off the paper. Quickly sprinkle all over with shredded lettuce and squirt a zig-zag of chilli sauce over lettuce. Roll up from the left side which will place the chicken in the centre of the roll. Cut in half with a diagonal cut. Wrap the end in a paper serviette and serve immediately.

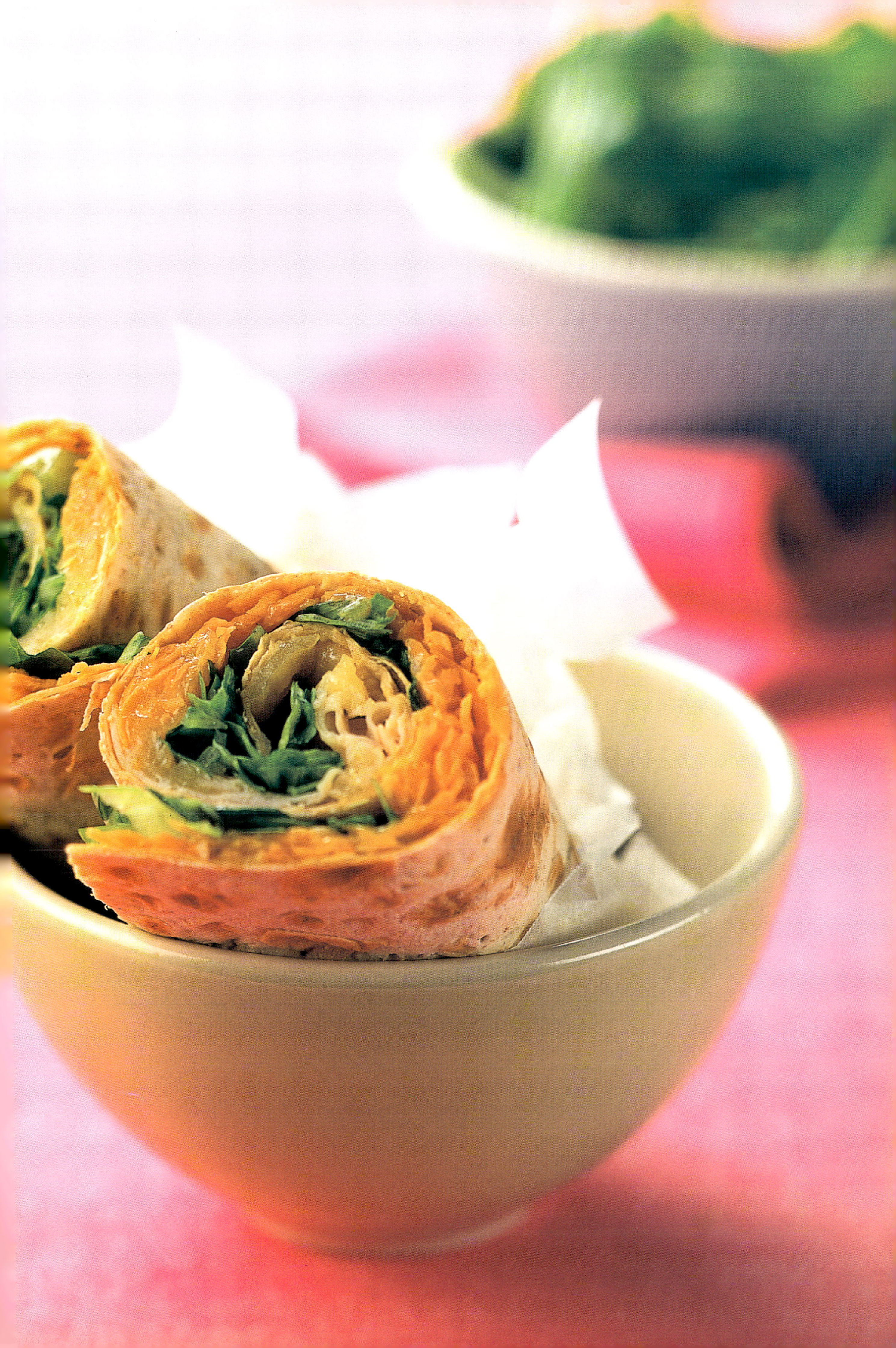

Turkey and Cranberry Bagels

GOURMET SANDWICHES AND FOCACCIA

Turkey and Cranberry Bagels

INGREDIENTS

2 fresh bagels

50g mascapone cheese

2 slices roast turkey breast

cranberry sauce

METHOD

1. Spread mascapone cheese on bagel halves, place on the turkey, cranberry sauce and top half of bagel.

2. Place in pre-heated **Sandwich Press** and cook for 2 minutes. Remove from press and brush top with a little cranberry sauce.

Salmon and Cream Cheese Focaccia

INGREDIENTS

1 slab focaccia bread, cut into 4 squares and split

250g cream cheese

1 piece preserved lemon, cut into thin strips

200g smoked salmon slices or strips

$3/4$ cup canned cucumbers, drained

METHOD

1. Spread both halves of each focaccio square with a layer of cream cheese and sprinkle with preserved lemon strips. Place the salmon onto the 4 bottom halves, cover with a few cucumber slices and close with remaining tops.

2. Place in pre-heated **Sandwich Press** and cook for 3 minutes.

GOURMET SANDWICHES AND FOCACCIA

Italian Style Focaccia

INGREDIENTS

1 tablespoon extra virgin olive oil

2 teaspoons balsamic vinegar

salt and MasterFoods Cracked Black Peppercorns to taste

4 slices grilled eggplant

6 slices grilled capsicum

1 quantity caramelised onion

1 rectangle focaccia slab cut into 4 portions

1 cup Mil Lel Shredded Parmesan Cheese

100g prosciutto (optional)

METHOD

1. Mix together the oil, vinegar and seasonings to make a dressing. Grill the eggplant, capsicum and onion as stated on pages 4 and 5. Place on a plate and drizzle with dressing, stand for 2 minutes.

2. Split the focaccia portions through the centre. On each base sprinkle a layer of shredded Parmesan, then stack on the eggplant, capsicum, prosciutto and cover with onions. Close with the focaccia tops.

3. Place in pre-heated **Sandwich Press** and cook 2 to 3 minutes. Open lid and sprinkle a layer of cheese on top and place on a strip of red capsicum. Cover with baking paper, close lid and cook 20 seconds. Carefully remove paper. Serve immediately with a garnish of rocket salad.

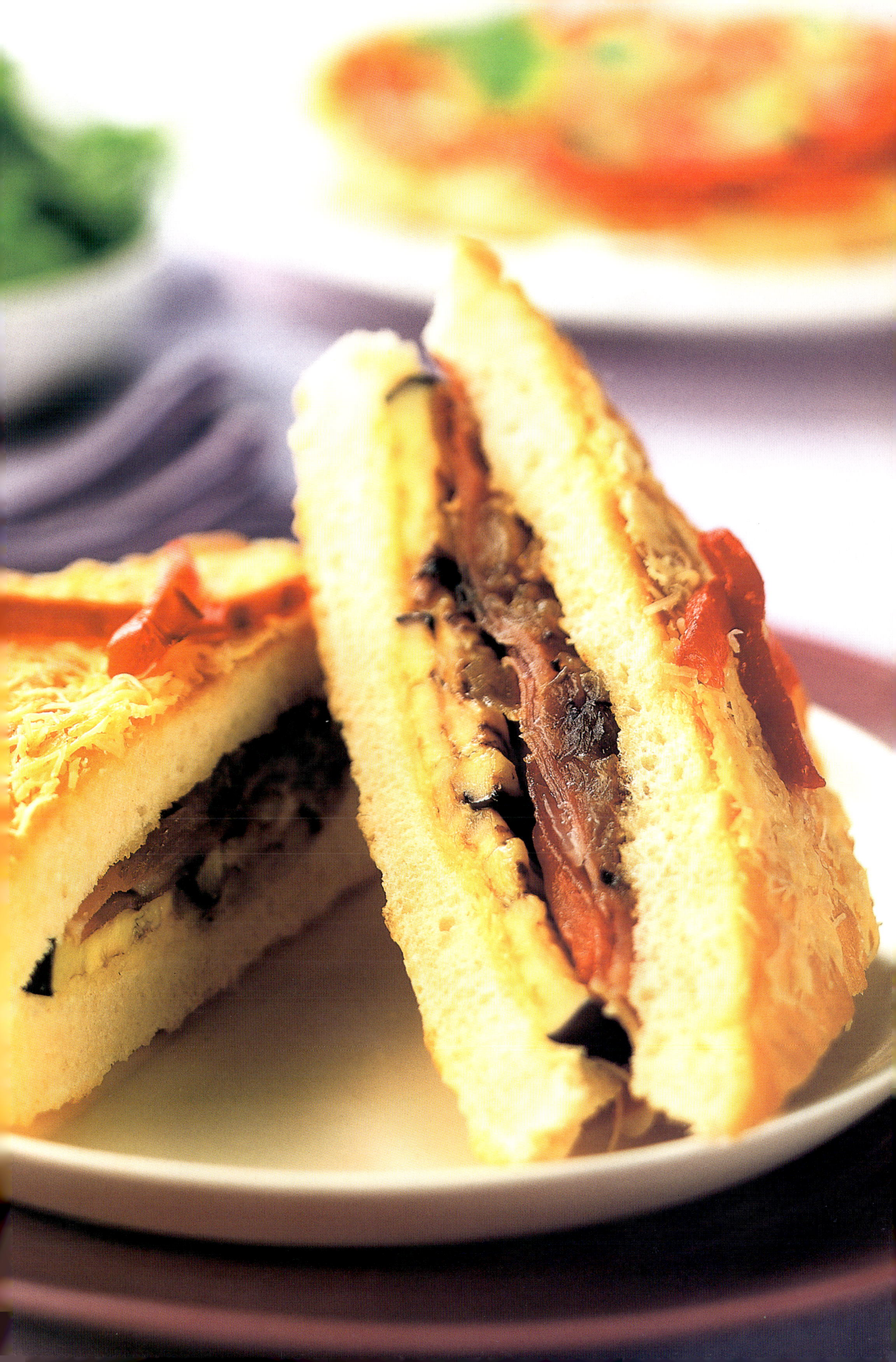

Grilled Chicken and Vegetable Focaccia

GOURMET SANDWICHES AND FOCACCIA

Grilled Chicken and Vegetable Focaccia

INGREDIENTS

6 chicken tenderloins

MasterFoods Garlic and Herb Salt

canola oil spray

2 x 15cm focaccia slab, cut into 4

2 sweet potatoes, sliced and grilled

2 zucchini, sliced and grilled

1 large onion, grilled

MasterFoods Freshly Blended Basil

50g semi-dried tomatoes

2 Fred Walker Swiss Cheese Slices

METHOD

1. Pound the chicken to flatten a little, sprinkle with garlic salt. Spray with oil and grill in the pre-heated **Sandwich Press** for about 2 minutes or until cooked. Grill the vegetables (see pages 4 and 5).

2. Spread a little basil on the Focaccia bases and fill with chicken, grilled vegetables, semi-dried tomatoes and cheese. Place in pre-heated **Sandwich Press** and cook for 3 minutes.

Turkey and Grilled Orange with Fennel on Pide

INGREDIENTS

canola oil spray

4 slices of orange

2 pieces fennel

4 long slices zucchini

2 oval Turkish pide buns

MasterFoods Lemon Tartare

2 large slices roast turkey breast

4 Fred Walker Swiss Cheese Slices

METHOD

1. Pre-heat the **Sandwich Press** and spray with oil. Grill the orange, fennel and zucchini with lid closed for 2 minutes or until done.

2. Split the pide buns, spread inside with lemon tartare. Assemble the Turkish pide sandwiches, placing in order the turkey, orange, fennel, zucchini and cheese. Cook for 3 minutes. Serve with salad garnish.

PIZZAS AND MELTS

A selection of open faced pizzas and melt No need to heat a large oven to make cheese snack. Use your favourite fillings o methods given below.

Pepperoni Tomato Pizza

INGREDIENTS

2 x 16cm Pizza bases (twin pack)

2 tablespoons MasterFoods Tomato and Chilli Pickle

6 small tomatoes, sliced

100g sliced pepperoni

salt and MasterFoods Italian Herbs, to taste

1 cup Mil Lel Shredded Mozzarella Cheese

½ cup fresh baby basil leaves

1 sheet baking paper

METHOD

1. Place the 2 pizza bases in the pre-heated **Sandwich Press**, close lid and heat for 2 minutes. Open lid, spread bases lightly with tomato and chilli pickle. Arrange overlapping tomato and peperoni slices around surfaces. Sprinkle with salt and herbs. Lower the lid for 30 seconds to heat the tomatoes.

2. Sprinkle cheese over both pizzas. Place a sheet of baking paper over the pizzas, close lid and cook for 20 to 30 seconds to melt the cheese. Remove paper. Sprinkle over basil leaves. Serve immediately.

which are quick to make in the **Sandwich Press.** pizza or heat a large grill to make a melted whatever you have on hand and follow the

Tomato and Basil Melts

PIZZAS AND MELTS

Tomato and Basil Melts

INGREDIENTS

2 slices sourdough bread, buttered
1 tablespoon MasterFoods Freshly Blended Basil
2 small Roma tomatoes, sliced
4 COON Tasty Natural Cheese Slices
1 sheet baking paper

METHOD

1. Pre-heat the **Sandwich Press**. Spread the basil on unbuttered side of bread and place in the **Sandwich Press** buttered side down for 1 minute with lid up, to toast the base.

2. Arrange the tomato slices on the bread and place 2 cheese slices onto each to cover surface. Cover with the baking paper, lower the lid, cook 15 to 20 seconds until cheese melts, remove paper. Serve immediately. Garnish with fresh basil leaves.

Tuna and Mushroom Pizza

INGREDIENTS

180g can of Tuna in brine, drained
2 teaspoons lemon juice
½ teaspoon MasterFoods Chopped Chives
½ teaspoon fresh dill
olive oil spray
1 large zucchini sliced into ½ cm thick rings
4 medium mushrooms, sliced
22cm packaged pizza base
½ cup MasterFoods Chunky Tomato Salsa
¾ cup Mil Lel Shredded Mozzarella Cheese
1 sheet baking paper

METHOD

1. Mix drained tuna with lemon juice, chives and dill. Pre-heat **Sandwich Press**, spray plates with oil then grill zucchini and mushroom slices. Remove and set aside.

2. Place the pizza base into the **Sandwich Press**, heat with lid down for about 2 minutes. Open lid and spread pizza base with salsa, top with zucchini, tuna and mushrooms and sprinkle with the mozzarella. Place sheet of baking paper over pizza, close lid to melt the cheese for 20 to 30 seconds. Remove paper and serve immediately.

PIZZAS AND MELTS

Roast Beef with Horseradish Cream

INGREDIENTS

2 slices Vienna bread, buttered

2 slices rare roast beef

2 teaspoons MasterFoods Horseradish Cream

2 small zucchini, thinly sliced

4 x 3mm slices Cracker Barrel Extra Sharp Vintage Cheddar Cheese cut from the end of the block

1 sheet of baking paper

METHOD

1. Pre-heat the **Sandwich Press**, place on the bread, buttered side down. Cook for 1 minute with lid up to toast the base.

2. Arrange roast beef slice on the bread, spread lightly with horseradish, cover with the zucchini and cheese. Place baking paper on top, close the lid and cook 20 to 25 seconds until cheese melts. Remove paper, serve immediately.

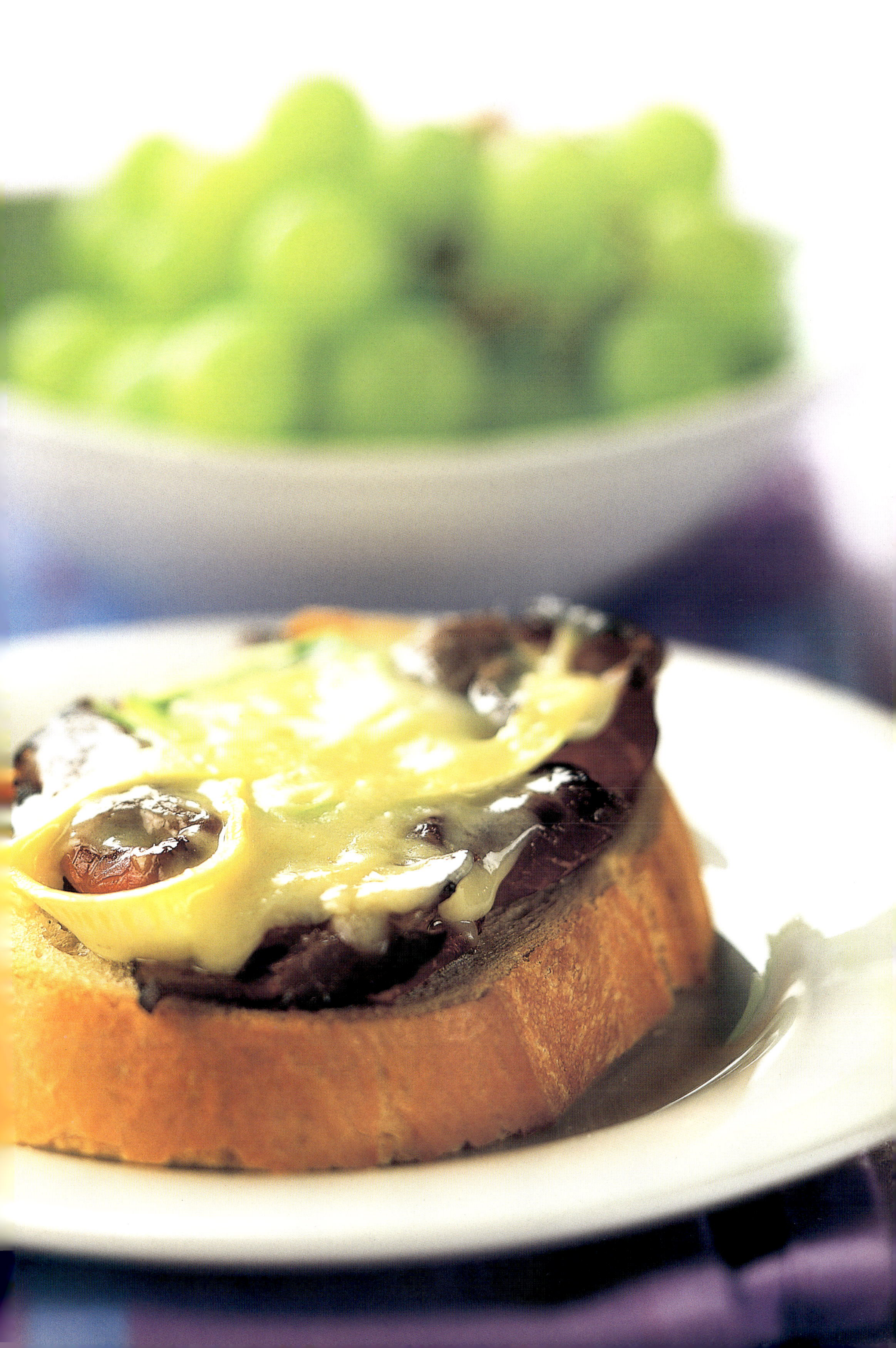

Unexpected guests are quickly catere

ENTERTAINING IDEAS

or with the aid of your **Sandwich Press.**

Bruschetta

These popular appetizers made with Italian ciabatta bread may be made with little effort in the **Sandwich Press**. For best results, use the "bake at home" ciabatta which is partly baked. Baking will be completed in the **Sandwich Press**, giving the correct crispness. Other Italian breads or French baguette may also be used.

INGREDIENTS

1 bake at home ciabatta loaf

olive oil spray

MasterFoods Garlic Bread Seasoning

TOPPING

1 punnet small cherry tomatoes, quartered

½ cup baby basil leaves

1 tablespoon garlic flavoured olive oil (see below)

METHOD

1. Cut 12 slices of ciabatta bread 2cm thick. Pre-heat **Sandwich Press**; spray the base plate with olive oil and place on the bread slices in 3 rows. Spray the bread with olive oil spray and sprinkle with garlic bread seasoning. Close the lid and cook about 2 minutes or until golden. Remove and arrange on a serving platter.

2. Pile the tomato and basil onto each slice and drizzle with a few drops of garlic oil. Serve immediately. Serve 3 to 4 pieces as an entrée.

> **Variations:**
> Pile on strips of smoked salmon, garnish with red caviar and a sprig of dill.
> Top with marinated capsicum strips and semi-dried tomatoes.
> **Garlic Flavoured Olive Oil:** Place 1 teaspoon MasterFoods Freshly Crushed Garlic into 1 cup extra virgin olive oil. Stand for 30 minutes before use.

ENTERTAINING IDEAS

Twelve melts can be made on the Sandwic ingredients prepared and ready to re-loac

Finger Food Melts

INGREDIENTS

1 baguette or French bread stick

butter oil spray or canola oil spray

3 tablespoons MasterFoods Chunky Mild Salsa

4 slices grilled eggplant, finely chopped

½ cup COON Tasty Natural Shredded Cheese

2 sheets baking paper cut to fit grill plate

METHOD

1. Cut, on the diagonal, 12 x 2cm (thick) slices of bread. Pre-heat the **Sandwich Press** and spray the base plate with oil spray. Arrange the bread on the base plate in 3 rows, spray tops of bread well with oil, close the lid and cook for 1½ minutes or until golden. Remove immediately.

2. Place a sheet of baking paper to line the base plate. Mix the salsa and eggplant together and spread onto each each slice of toast. Place toast sliceson **Sandwich Press**, close together. Sprinkle the shredded cheese all over the top of the toast (the paper will catch the spills). Cover with the second sheet of paper, close the lid and cook for 20 seconds. Lift lid, carefully peel off paper. Arrange on platter and serve immediately.

Variations: Spread with MasterFoods Tomato and Chilli Pickle or Corn Relish, top with any shaved deli meats, sprinkle with cheese and melt.

ress. If more are required, have all they take only 2 minutes to cook.

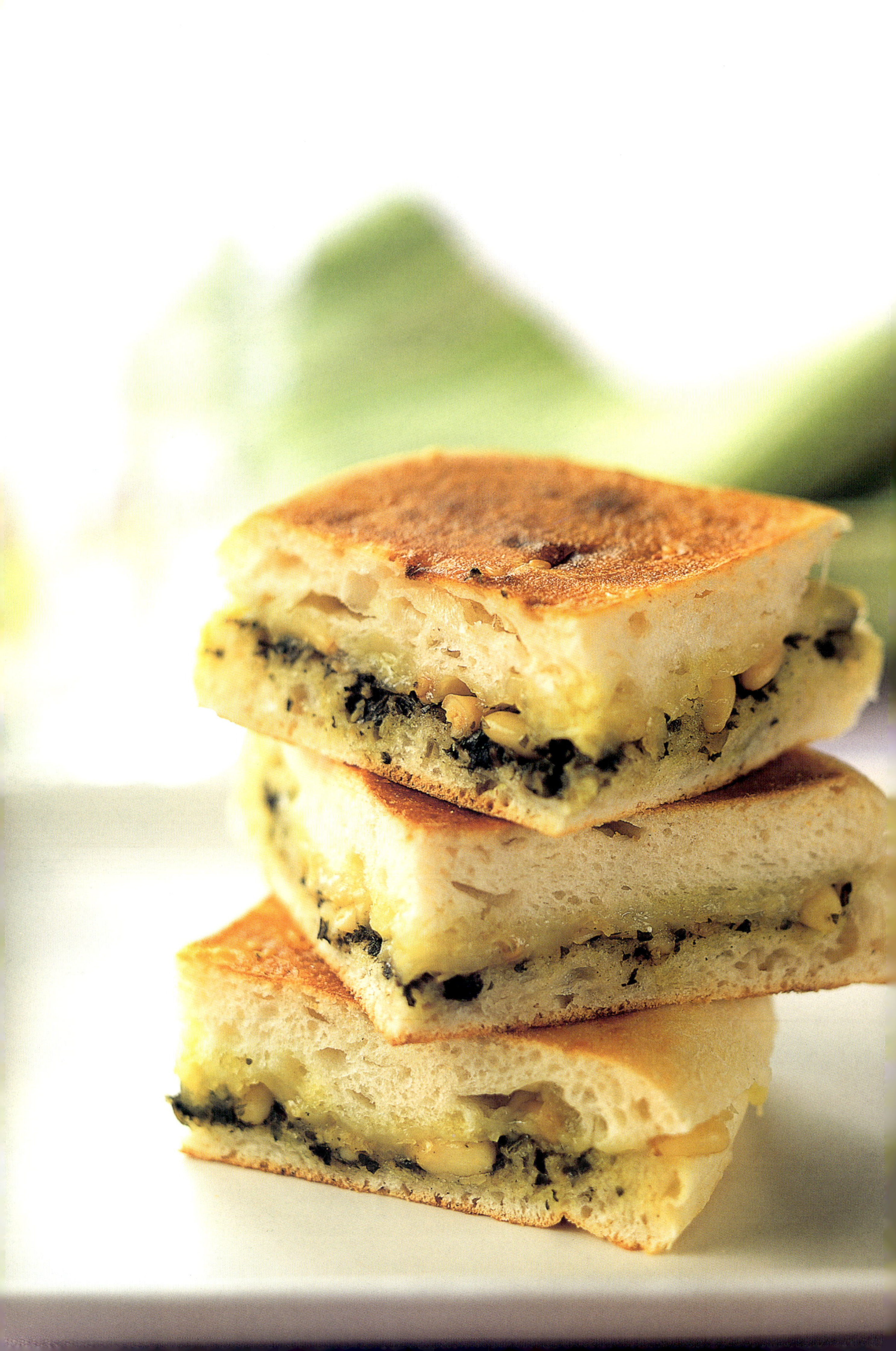

ENTERTAINING IDEAS

Pesto Cheese Triangles

INGREDIENTS

2 round Turkish pide buns

2 tablespoons MasterFoods Freshly Blended Basil

3 tablespoons pine nuts

½ cup Mil Lel Shredded Mozzarella Cheese

¼ cup Mil Lel Shredded Parmesan Cheese

canola oil spray

METHOD

1. Split the buns crosswise into 2 halves. Spread base half of each with the basil and sprinkle with pine nuts. Mix the 2 cheeses together and spread half on each. Place on the top half.

2. Pre-heat the **Sandwich Press**, spray the base plate with oil. Place on the pide buns, close lid and cook for 4 minutes or until crisp. Remove, cut each half with a sharp knife into 8 triangles. Serve warm.

THE JAFFLE MAKER

The deep recess of the **Jaffle Maker** will take a substantial filling, creating a hearty snack or quick meal. The filling is completely enclosed in the bread and all edges are sealed. Moist fillings are particularly suited to the **Jaffle Maker**. Puff and Shortcrust pastry may also be used, giving the opportunity to create delicious quick sweets.

JAFFLE SNACKS

Roast Pumpkin Snack

INGREDIENTS

1 cup roast pumpkin, mashed

2 tablespoons chopped onion

1 teaspoon MasterFoods Chopped Chives

½ teaspoon MasterFoods Ground Nutmeg

salt to taste

¼ teaspoon MasterFoods Ground Black Peppercorns

2 tablespoons cooked green peas

⅓ cup Mil Lel Shredded Parmesan Cheese

4 slices sandwich bread, buttered

METHOD

1. Mix all filling ingredients together. Divide in 2 and spread thickly on unbuttered side of 2 bread slices, top with bread slice, buttered side up.

2. Pre-heat **Jaffle Maker**, place in the sandwiches, close lid and cook for 3 minutes. Remove and serve.

Tip: Roast extra pumpkin when cooking a baked dinner to set aside for snacks. Boiled or mashed pumpkin may also be used.

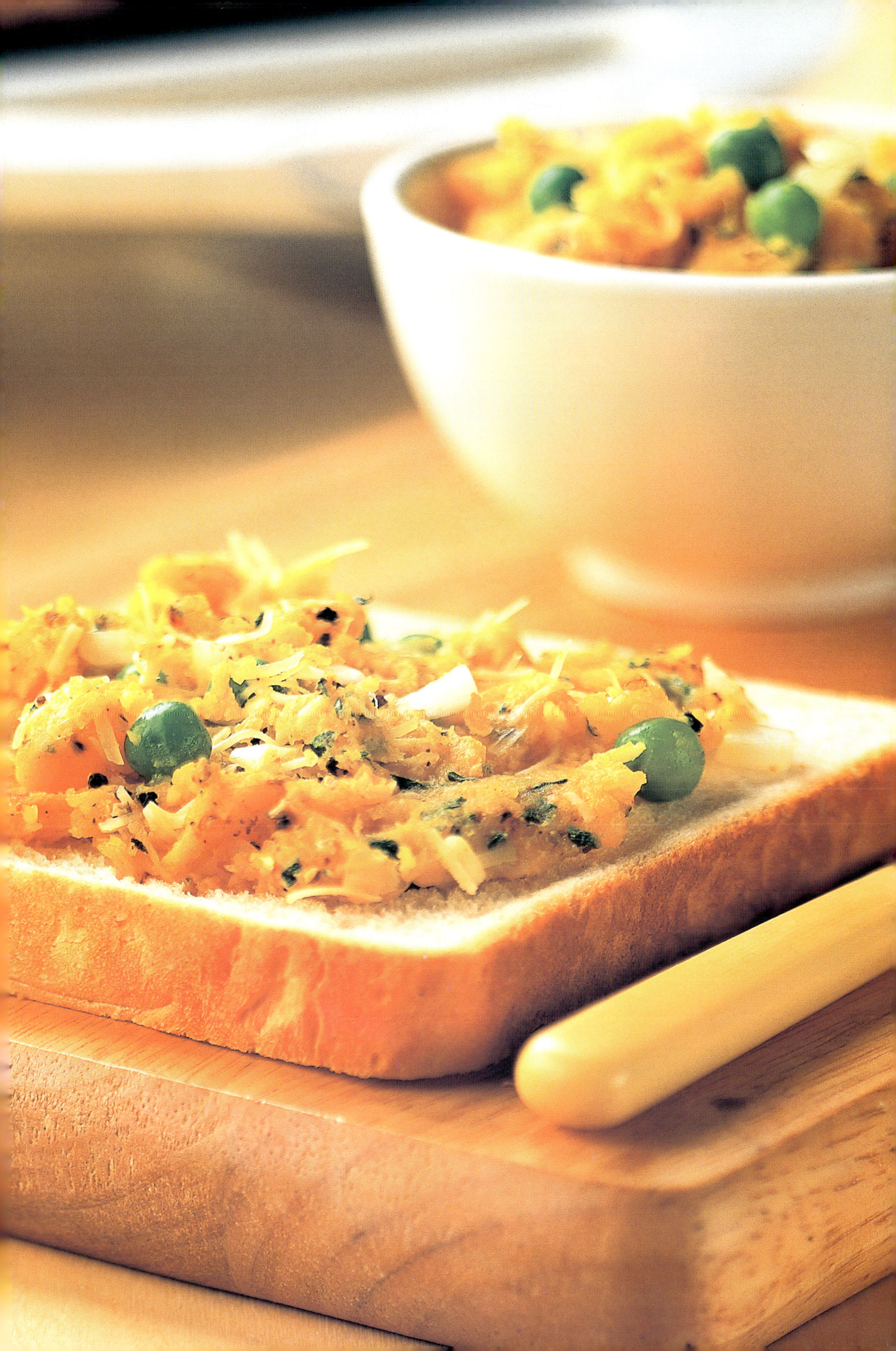

JAFFLE SNACKS

Salmon or Tuna Snack

INGREDIENTS

210g can red salmon or tuna

½ teaspoon MasterFoods Freshly Crushed Garlic

1 medium tomato, seeded and diced

2 tablespoons finely chopped red onion

½ cup COON Tasty Natural Shredded Cheese

1 tablespoon MasterFoods Seafood Cocktail Sauce

4 slices sandwich bread, buttered

METHOD

1. Mix all filling ingredients together. Divide in 2 and spread thickly onto unbuttered side of two bread slices; top with bread slice buttered side up.

2. Pre-heat the **Jaffle Maker**, place in the sandwiches and close the lid. Cook 3 to 4 minutes until golden. Remove and serve.

Roast Lamb and Vegetables

INGREDIENTS

¾ cup cold roast lamb, chopped

½ cup mixed vegetables (left overs)

1 small onion, finely chopped

½ teaspoon MasterFoods Lamb Herbs

2 tablespoons gravy

4 slices sandwich bread, buttered

METHOD

1. Mix all filling ingredients together. Divide in 2 and spread thickly onto unbuttered side of two bread slices; top with bread slice buttered side up.

2. Pre-heat the **Jaffle Maker**, place in the sandwiches and close the lid. Cook 3 to 4 minutes until golden. Remove and serve.

Note: This is a good way to serve left overs if cooking a lamb roast. For variation, add ¼ teaspoon MasterFoods Curry Powder.

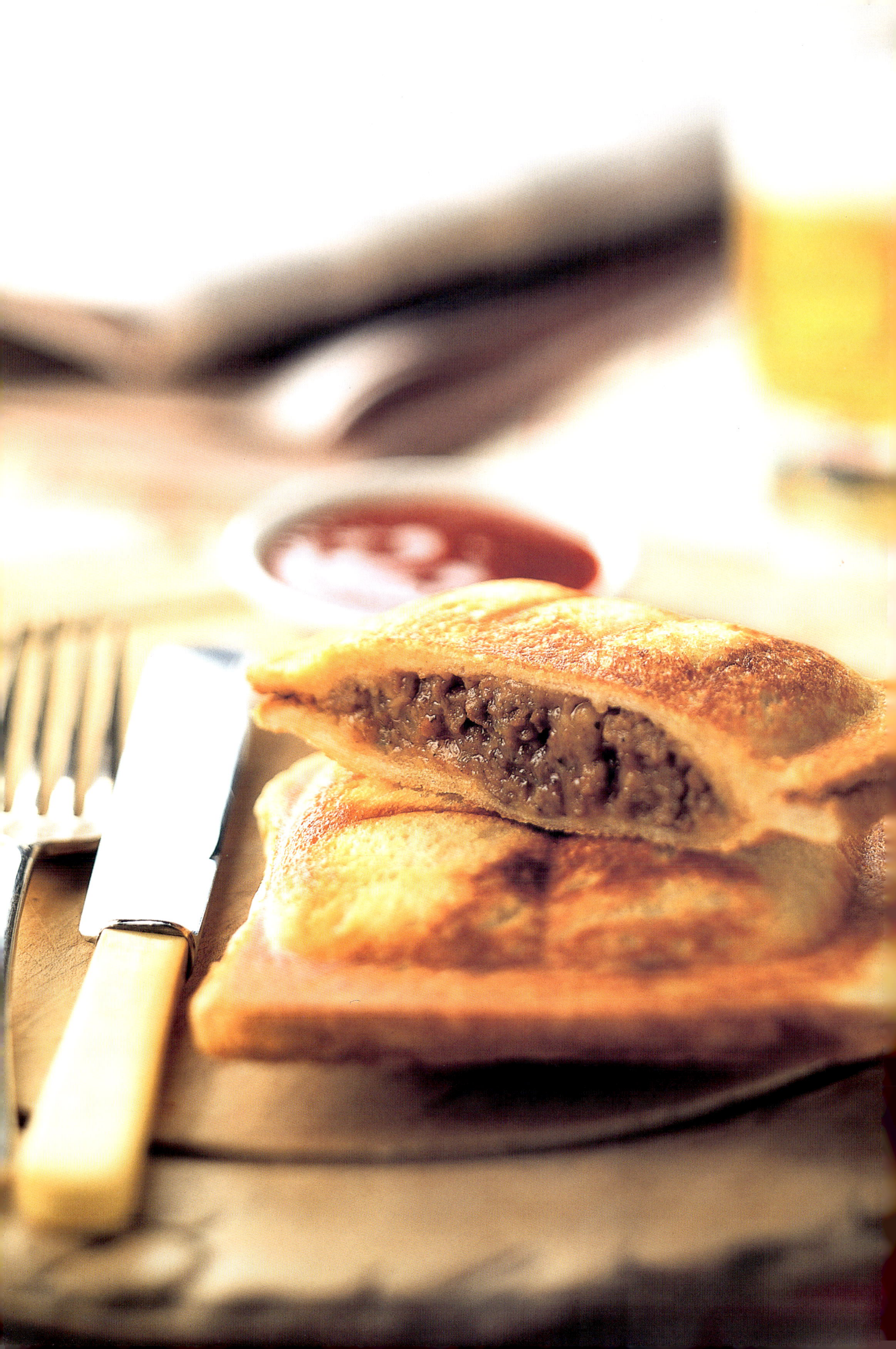

JAFFLE SNACKS

Tasty Aussie Pie

INGREDIENTS

1 tablespoon oil

1 small onion, finely chopped

125g lean minced beef

½ teaspoon MasterFoods Garlic and Herb Salt

¼ teaspoon MasterFoods Ground Black Peppercorns

¼ teaspoon MasterFoods Ground Nutmeg

1 tablespoon MasterFoods Tomato Sauce

½ cup Mil Lel Shredded Parmesan Cheese

1 small egg, beaten

4 slices sandwich bread, buttered

METHOD

1. Heat oil in a small pan and fry the onion. Add mince, stir to brown breaking up any lumps. Reduce heat and add salt, pepper, nutmeg and sauce. Simmer for 15 minutes, adding a drop of water if necessary. Remove to a bowl to cool, then add egg and cheese.

2. Pre-heat **Jaffle Maker**, place 2 bread slices, buttered side down into both recesses. Spoon in the mince filling and place second slice, buttered side up, on top. Close lid and cook for 4 minutes. Serve immediately.

Cheese Topping: A cheese topping will enhance the look of any snack. When snack is cooked, open lid and sprinkle tops with Mil Lel Shredded Parmesan Cheese. Place a piece of baking paper on top and close the lid for 10 to 20 seconds. Remove paper and serve.

Note: This is a great way to serve left-over bolognaise sauce. Simply add cheese and egg to your bolognaise sauce and follow step two in the method above.

JAFFLE SNACKS

Spinach Pie

INGREDIENTS

250g packet frozen English spinach, thawed

3 shallots, finely chopped

1 teaspoon MasterFoods Chopped Dill

150g Australian Farmers Feta Cheese, crumbled

½ cup Mil Lel Shredded Parmesan Cheese

salt to taste

¼ teaspoon MasterFoods Ground Black Peppercorns

¼ teaspoon MasterFoods Ground Nutmeg

1 large egg

4 sheets filo pastry

olive or canola oil spray

METHOD

1. Place the thawed spinach in a strainer and press out all the water using the back of a wooden spoon. Place in a bowl and mix in the remaining filling ingredients.

2. Place 1 sheet of filo pastry on work surface (keep remainder covered). Spray lightly with oil spray. Fold the short side over towards the other side leaving ⅓ uncovered, then fold remaining ⅓ back over to cover. Spray with oil and fold front edge to back. Repeat with remaining 3 sheets. You now have 4 squares of filo 12cm x 13cm.

3. Place a square of filo into each recess of the **Jaffle Maker**. Spoon in the filling and cover with a square of filo. Close the lid and turn on the power. Cook for 10 to 12 minutes. Serve immediately with tomato and cucumber salad.

Ham and Egg Pie

INGREDIENTS

70g ham slices

MasterFoods Tomato Mustard

2 tablespoons Mil Lel Shredded Parmesan Cheese

2 eggs

1 sheet frozen puff pastry cut into 4 even squares, thawed

salt and pepper to taste

METHOD

1. Pre-heat the **Jaffle Maker**. Place a pastry square in each recess. Place half the ham into each, squirt with Tomato Mustard to liking, sprinkle with cheese then break an egg into each. Sprinkle with salt and pepper to taste. Place on the pastry tops and close the lid. Cook for 10 to 12 minutes.

2. Serve immediately.

Note: The egg may be beaten before adding if desired, but a whole cooked egg enclosed in pastry looks inviting.

Ham and Egg Pie

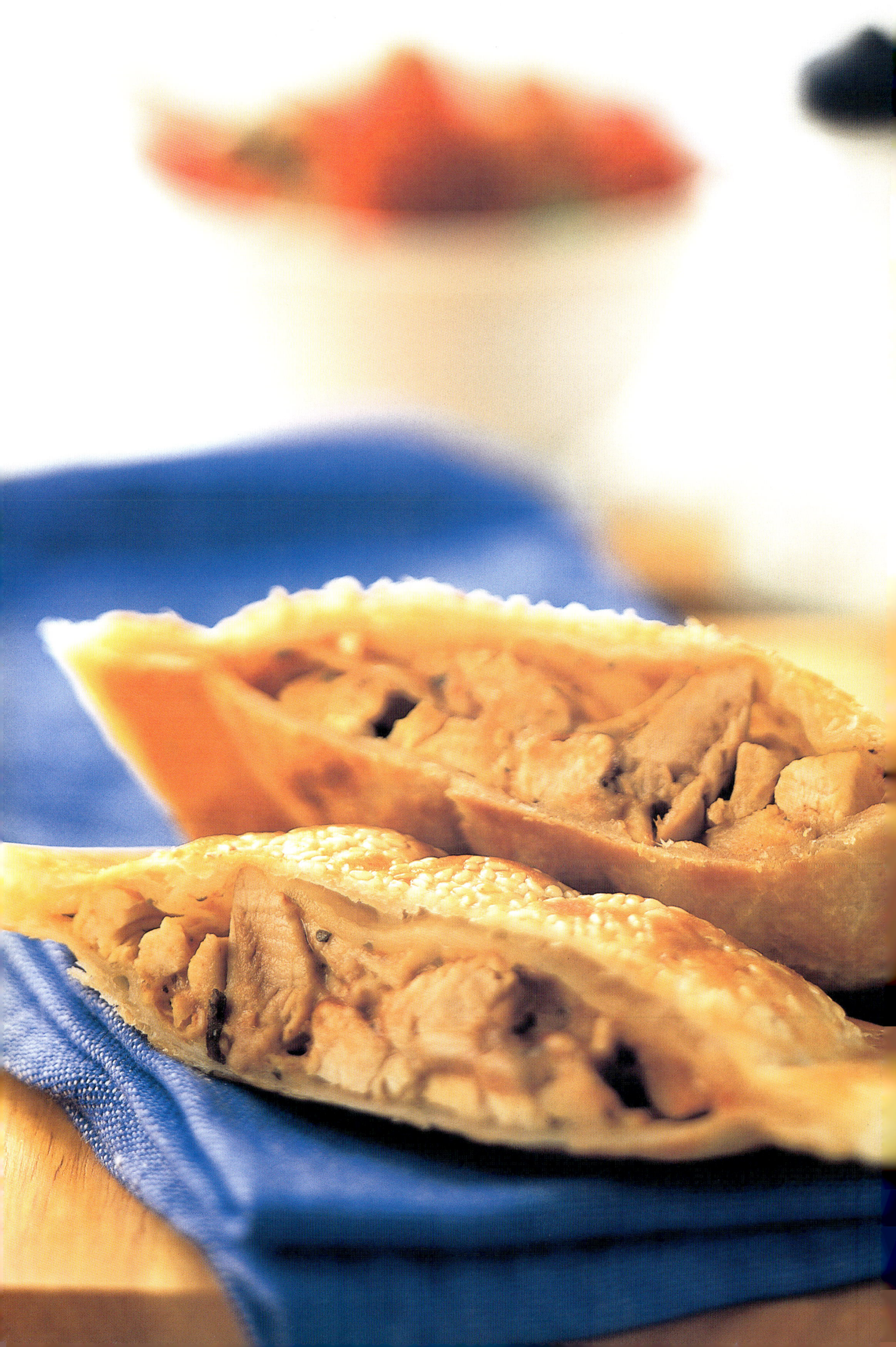

JAFFLE SNACKS

Chicken and Vegetable Pie

INGREDIENTS

1½ cups cooked chicken, shredded

2 tablespoons MasterFoods Corn Relish

¼ cup Mil Lel Shredded Mozzarella Cheese

1 sheet frozen puff pastry cut into 4 even squares, thawed

milk to glaze

2 teaspoons MasterFoods Sesame Seeds

METHOD

1. Mix chicken, corn relish and cheese together.
2. Pre-heat the **Jaffle Maker**. Place a pastry square into each recess, divide filling and spoon into each recess then top with pastry square. Glaze with a little milk, sprinkle with sesame seeds and close the lid. Cook for 10 to 12 minutes. Remove and serve hot.

JAFFLE SNACKS

Quick pies can be cooked in the Jaffle

Herbed Ham Pie

INGREDIENTS

100ml Dairy Farmers Sour Cream

1 egg

2½ tablespoons chopped ham (about 40g)

2 teaspoons MasterFoods Herb Mustard with Garlic

2 teaspoons MasterFoods Chopped Chives

2 tablespoons COON Tasty Natural Shredded Cheese

1 sheet frozen puff pastry cut into 4 even squares, thawed

METHOD

1. Place sour cream and egg into a small bowl and beat until well combined. Stir in the ham, mustard, chives and cheese.

2. Pre-heat the **Jaffle Maker.** Place a pastry square into each recess. Divide filling and spoon into each recess, then top with pastry square and close the lid. Cook for 10 minutes.

Turn off heat and leave 2 minutes more if needed to set the centre. Remove, serve hot with salad garnish.

Salmon Pie

INGREDIENTS

100ml Dairy Farmers Sour Cream

1 egg

1 teaspoon MasterFoods Tomato Mustard

110g can red salmon, flaked

1 teaspoon MasterFoods Chopped Parsley

1 teaspoon lemon juice

2 tablespoons COON Tasty Natural Shredded Cheese

salt and pepper to taste

1 sheet frozen puff pastry cut into 4 even squares, thawed

METHOD

1. Mix sour cream, egg and mustard together. Stir in the salmon, parsley, lemon juice, cheese and seasonings.

2. Pre-heat the **Jaffle Maker.** Place a pastry square into each recess. Divide filling and spoon into each recess, then top with pastry square and close the lid. Cook for 10 minutes. Remove and serve hot with salad garnish.

Variation: You can also make quick quiches. Simply follow the method above, but do not place pastry squares on top. For this variation you only need ½ sheet frozen puff pastry cut into 2 even squares.

Maker. Serve with a salad for a light lunch.

Salmon Pie

SWEETS

Delicious sweets can be made in the Jaffl
to satisfy your craving.

Fresh Apple Pie

INGREDIENTS

375g packet frozen short crust pastry

1 large red apple, cored and finely diced

1 tablespoon caster sugar

2 tablespoons sultanas

½ teaspoon MasterFoods Cinnamon

METHOD

1. Cut the block of frozen pastry in half. Let one half stand to defrost and place remaining half back in freezer for future use.

2. Meanwhile prepare filling. Core the apple and dice finely. Mix with remaining ingredients.

3. Roll pastry thinly on a lightly floured board and cut into 4 squares measuring 13cm by 11cm.

4. Pre-heat the **Jaffle Maker**. Place a square of pastry in each recess, divide filling equally and spoon into each recess, then top with pastry. Brush top of pie with water and sprinkle with sugar. Close the lid and cook for 10 minutes. Serve with whipped cream.

Maker. No need to heat a large oven

Apple Charlotte

SWEETS

Apple Charlotte

INGREDIENTS

1 cup canned pie apple

2 tablespoons caster sugar

1½ tablespoons MasterFoods Passionfruit Butter

4 slices sultana or spiced fruit bread, buttered

METHOD

1. Mix filling ingredients together.
2. Preheat the **Jaffle Maker**. Place 2 slices bread, buttered side down in each recess, spoon in equal amount of filling, cover with top slices buttered side up.

Close the lid and cook 4 minutes. Serve with thickened cream.

Quick Cheese Cake

INGREDIENTS

125g cream cheese, at room temperature

2 tablespoons caster sugar

1 tablespoon MasterFoods Lemon Butter

1 sheet frozen puff pastry, thawed

½ cup whipped Dairy Farmers Cream

fruit for garnish

METHOD

1. Mix cream cheese, sugar and lemon butter well together.
2. Cut 2 squares of puff pastry 13cmx11cm.
3. Pre-heat the **Jaffle Maker**, quickly place the pastry into each recess. Spoon in an equal amount of cream cheese mixture into each and close the lid. Cook 8 minutes, turn off the power and leave in the **Jaffle Maker** for 2 minutes. Remove and chill in refrigerator, garnish with whipped cream and fresh fruit.

SWEETS

Bread and Butter Custard

INGREDIENTS

1 tablespoon plain flour

2 teaspoons butter

1 tablespoon sugar

1 teaspoon MasterFoods Vanilla Sugar

1 egg

¾ cup Dairy Farmers Milk

4 slices fruit and spice loaf, buttered

2 teaspoons icing sugar

METHOD

1. Place flour, butter, sugar and egg into a small saucepan, mix quickly together and stir in the milk. Stir over heat until mixture thickens and boils. Cool slightly.

2. Preheat the **Jaffle Maker**. Place 2 bread slices, buttered side down, into each recess and pour in an equal amount of custard into each. Cover with remaining bread slices, buttered side up and close the lid. Cook for 4 minutes. Dust with icing sugar. Serve warm with a berry sauce.

Peach and Almond Tart

INGREDIENTS

1 egg

1½ tablespoons caster sugar

1 tablespoon Dairy Farmers Cream

2 tablespoons almond meal

½ sheet frozen puff pastry, thawed

2 canned peach halves

1 tablespoon almond flakes

1 piece baking paper

thickened cream to serve

METHOD

1. Beat egg, sugar and cream together and stir in the almond meal.

2. Cut the pastry into 2 even squares 13cm x 11cm. Place into the pre-heated **Jaffle Maker**. Place a peach half into centre of each square and spoon the almond mixture around the peach leaving top exposed.

3. Sprinkle flaked almonds on pastry edge and almond mixture. Cover with the baking paper, close the lid and cook 12 minutes. Remove the paper

4. Serve warm with cream.

Variation: Pear halves or stewed prunes may also be used.

Bread and Butter Custard

THE SANDWICH MAKER

Introduction

The **Sandwich Maker** will toast the sandwiches to perfection, cut them into 2 triangles and seal all edges enclosing the filling. The sealed sandwiches are easy to make and fun to eat. They are a winner for weekend and holiday lunches; children love them and enjoy sharing them with their friends.

METHOD OF MAKING SEALED SANDWICHES IN THE SANDWICH MAKER

1. Spread the bread on one side with softened butter or margarine.

2. Spread on or assemble the fillings on the unbuttered side of the bread and close the sandwich with bread slice, buttered side up.

3. Pre-heat the Sandwich Maker. When green light turns on, place in the sandwiches, making sure that they sit neatly into the recess. Close the lid and click the latch into position. Cook for 3 to 4 minutes. Remove with the aid of a plastic spatula. Allow to cool a little before eating as some fillings retain heat and can burn if eaten immediately.

Note: For low-fat sandwiches, assemble and close with unbuttered bread. Spray the base plate of the **Sandwich Maker** with canola or olive oil spray, place in the sandwiches and spray the tops lightly with oil spray.
Breads Suitable for the Sandwich Maker are Standard and super size white sandwich bread; white, wholemeal, rye, wholegrain, soy and linseed, sourdough. Loaf breads of any variety may also be used.

FILLING COMBINATIONS FOR THE SANDWICH MAKER

Fillings may be simple or exotic or last night's left overs. Chopped ingredients, which may be difficult to contain in a flat sandwich, are better suited to the sealed toasted sandwich. Layered sliced fillings may also be used. Moist foods such as left over savoury mince or stew, or cooked vegetable mixtures work very well as the bread soaks in the juices. Take care however, not to overfill as the sandwiches may leak during cooking.

Quantities

All quantities are for four (4) sandwiches which yields 8 triangles. For the 2 recess Sandwich Maker, just halve the quantity. If using the 4 recess Sandwich Maker and you only wish to make 2 sandwiches, it is all right to leave 2 compartments empty.

Simple Toasted Sandwiches as above may also be made in a floating hinge snackmaker such as the Sandwich Press.

Selection of Apricot Chicken, Baked Beans and Apple and tasty Ham, Swiss Cheese and Tomato Snacks. See pages 76-77.

FILLING COMBINATIONS FOR THE SANDWICH MAKER

Apricot Chicken

INGREDIENTS

1½ cups chopped cooked chicken

½ cup chopped dried apricots

2 tablespoons light mayonnaise

1 teaspoon MasterFoods Dijonnaise Mustard

8 slices buttered sandwich bread of your choice

METHOD

1. Mix filling ingredients together. Assemble and cook as directed on page 74.

Bacon and Pineapple

INGREDIENTS

100g diced bacon pieces

¾ cup Mil Lel Shredded Mozzarella Cheese

½ x 225g can pineapple pieces, drained

8 slices buttered sandwich bread of your choice

METHOD

1. Mix filling ingredients together. Assemble and cook as directed on page 74.

Prawn Cocktail

INGREDIENTS

250g cooked shelled prawns, chopped

3 fresh shallots, finely chopped

1 cup COON Tasty Natural Shredded Cheese

3 tablespoons MasterFoods Seafood Cocktail Sauce

8 slices buttered bread of your choice

METHOD

1. Mix filling ingredients together. Assemble and cook as directed on page 74.

Prune, Walnut and Tasty Cheese

INGREDIENTS

½ cup chopped pitted prunes

½ cup chopped walnuts

1 cup COON Tasty Natural Shredded Cheese

8 slices buttered sandwich bread of your choice

METHOD

1. Mix filling ingredients together. Assemble and cook as directed on page 74.

Ham, Swiss Cheese and Tomato

INGREDIENTS

4 slices smoked ham

1 tablespoon MasterFoods Honey Wholegrain Mustard

2 medium tomatoes, sliced

4 Fred Walker Swiss Cheese Slices

8 slices buttered sandwich bread of your choice

METHOD

1. Assemble and cook as directed on page 74.

Baked Beans and Apple

INGREDIENTS

350g can baked beans

2 medium red apples, peeled cored and diced

½ cup Mil Lel Shredded Parmesan Cheese

8 slices buttered sandwich bread of your choice

METHOD

1. Mix filling ingredients together. Assemble and cook as directed on page 74.

Potato Mash Supreme

INGREDIENTS

1 cup cold mashed potato

1 large onion, finely chopped and fried until golden

½ cup cooked baby peas

½ teaspoon MasterFoods Freshly Crushed Garlic

½ cup chopped sun dried tomatoes

½ cup Mil Lel Shredded Parmesan Cheese

salt to taste

MasterFoods Ground Black Peppercorns to taste

8 slices buttered sandwich bread of your choice

METHOD

1. Mix all filling ingredients together. Assemble and cook as directed on page 74.

Selection of Apricot Chicken, Baked Beans and Apple, and tasty Ham, Swiss Cheese and Tomato snacks.

Salmon Salad

INGREDIENTS

210g can red salmon, drained

½ teaspoon MasterFoods Freshly Crushed Garlic

3 shallots, chopped

1 tablespoon chopped gherkin

½ cup COON Tasty Natural Shredded Cheese

2 tablespoons MasterFoods Lemon Tartare Sauce

8 slices buttered sandwich bread of your choice

METHOD

1. Mix all filling ingredients together. Assemble and cook as directed on page 74.

Sweet and Sour Chicken

FILLING COMBINATIONS FOR THE SANDWICH MAKER

Sweet and Sour Chicken

INGREDIENTS

1½ cups shredded cooked chicken

½ cup coarsely grated carrot

½ green capsicum, diced

3 shallots, chopped

salt to taste

MasterFoods Ground Black Peppercorns to taste

2 tablespoons MasterFoods Sweet and Sour Sauce

8 slices buttered bread of your choice

METHOD

1. Mix all filling ingredients together. Assemble and cook as directed on page 74.

Sausage Sizzle

INGREDIENTS

3 barbequed sausages, thinly sliced

2 small onions, thinly sliced

3 medium mushrooms, sliced

MasterFoods Barbeque Sauce or Tomato Sauce

8 slices buttered bread of your choice

METHOD

1. Assemble and cook as directed on page 74.

> All of the above recipes can also be made in the deeper snackmaker; the Jaffle Maker. As the recess is much deeper than the triangular Sandwich Maker, the given quantities will make 2 jaffles.

ENTERTAINERS

Your **Sandwich Maker** can be used t

Nacho Platter

Easy to make, fun to eat. Serve at teenage gatherings or TV Footy Parties. The quantities given will produce 24 triangles.

INGREDIENTS

420g can MasterFoods Mexican Chilli Beans

1 cup COON Tasty Natural Shredded Cheese

1 loaf super sized sandwich bread, buttered

1 jar MasterFoods Guacamole Dip

300ml carton Dairy Farmers Sour Cream

1 bottle MasterFoods Sweet Chilli Sauce

METHOD

1. Mix the Mexican chilli beans and shredded cheese together. Line up 4 slices of bread, buttered side down and spoon 2 heaped tablespoons of bean mixture into each slice. Place on the top slice, buttered side up; do not press down.

2. Carefully place into the pre-heated Sandwich Maker, close the lid and click the latch. Cook for 4 minutes. Meanwhile prepare the next 4 sandwiches and continue likewise until all are cooked.

3. Arrange on a large tray with bowls of guacamole and sour cream for dipping and a squeeze bottle of sweet chilli sauce as an extra choice.

produce food for a small crowd.

**Serve these deliciou
include in a chees**

ENTERTAINERS

riangles with a glass of chilled white wine, or
and fruit platter.

Blue Vein Cheese and Date Triangles

INGREDIENTS

150g Fred Walker Blue Vein Cheese

10 pitted dates, finely chopped

8 slices white sandwich bread

METHOD

1. Mix the blue vein cheese and chopped dates together. Spread on the unbuttered side of 4 slices of bread and close with remaining slices, buttered side up.

2. Place in the pre-heated **Sandwich Maker** and cook for 3 minutes. Remove and allow to cool slightly before cutting each triangle in half. Makes 16 small triangles.

Variation: 2 frozen puff pastry sheets may be used in place of bread. Cut each sheet into 4 equal pieces, roll the edges on the left and right side to extend to the appropriate size to fit the recess.
Pre-heat the Sandwich Maker, place in the 4 base pieces and spoon the filling into the triangular recesses. Cover with the top piece and close the lid.
Cook for 8 minutes.

Note: *The recess measures 13cm x 11½cm, so roll the square of pastry to fit.*

ENTERTAINERS

To accompany happy hour drinks o

Cheese Triangles with Filo Pastry

INGREDIENTS

125g Australian Farmer's Feta Cheese, crumbled

3 tablespoons Mil Lel Shredded Parmesan Cheese

1 tablespoon semolina

2 eggs

1 teaspoon MasterFoods Parsley Flakes or Chives

¼ teaspoon MasterFoods Ground Black Peppercorns

¼ teaspoon MasterFoods Ground Nutmeg

7 sheets filo pastry

olive or canola oil spray

sprinkle of MasterFoods Sesame Seeds

METHOD

1. Mix the cheeses, semolina, eggs and flavourings together.

2. Place the stack of 7 sheets of filo on a cutting board with the long side in front of you. Cut a 12cm strip off one end and set aside for other use.

3. From the stack take one sheet and spray with oil, place second sheet on top and spray, repeat with the third sheet. Repeat the process to make another pile of four sheets.

4. Place the 3 sheet pile onto the base plate of the COLD **Sandwich Maker**, easing into the triangle recesses without tearing. Spoon the cheese mixture carefully into each triangle recess. Place the 4 sheet pile over the top. Spray with oil and sprinkle surface with sesame seeds. Close the lid, click the latch and turn on the power to heat. Cook for 10 to 12 minutes.

5. To remove, slide onto a tray then place on cutting board. Cut and trim on the markings. Serve immediately. Makes 8 triangles.

erve as an entrée with a salad garnish.

Quick Custard Pie

SWEET TREATS

Quick Custard Pie

INGREDIENTS

¾ cup Dairy Farmers Custard

1 egg

2 tablespoons semolina

2 tablespoons caster sugar

1 teaspoon MasterFoods Vanilla Sugar (optional)

2 sheets frozen puff pastry, thawed

1 tablespoon icing sugar mixed with 1 teaspoon MasterFoods Ground Cinnamon

METHOD

1. Mix the first five ingredients together and place in a jug. Stand 10 minutes for the semolina to swell.

2. Cut each sheet of puff pastry into 4 equal squares. Roll to extend the size as given in step 2 in previous recipe.

3. Pre-heat the **Sandwich Maker** and place a square of pastry into each compartment, with the wider edge to front; press into the recess. Pour the custard into each triangular recess to come almost to the top of the recess. Cover with pastry tops and close the lid. Press lid down tightly and hold with your hand for a few seconds. <u>Do **not** clip the latch in place.</u> The lid will rise during cooking as the custard swells. Cook for 10 to 12 minutes.

4. Remove by sliding onto a tray then onto cutting board. Trim edges and separate the triangles. Place on wire cooler and sprinkle with icing sugar and cinnamon. Allow to cool, then serve warm.

Fresh Apple Triangles

INGREDIENTS

2 large or 3 medium red apples

1½ tablespoons sultanas

1½ tablespoons caster sugar

½ teaspoon MasterFoods Ground Cinnamon

2 sheets frozen puff pastry, thawed

1 tablespoon icing sugar

METHOD

1. Peel the apples, cut and remove core then dice finely. Mix the diced apple, sultanas, sugar and cinnamon together.

2. Cut each sheet of pastry into 4 equal squares. On a lightly floured board roll out each square with a rolling pin to extend each side, making the square 13cm by 13cm (to fit the recess).

3. Pre-heat the **Sandwich Maker** and place pastry into each compartment, with wider edge to the front. Spoon the apple filling into each triangular recess and cover with pastry top. Close the lid and click the latch. Cook for 10 minutes.

4. Remove carefully to cutting board and trim through the markings, cutting off excess. Sprinkle with icing sugar. Allow to cool, then serve warm. Serve with whipped cream.

SWEET TREATS

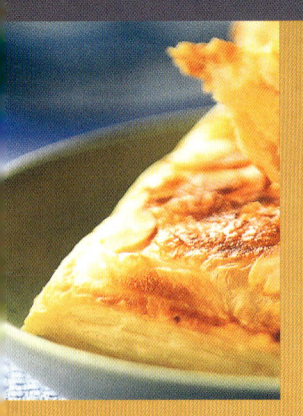

Apricot and Almond Puffs

INGREDIENTS

1 tablespoon butter, softened

1½ tablespoons caster sugar

6 tablespoons (65g) almond meal

8 dried apricots, coarsely chopped

60g egg, lightly beaten

2 sheets frozen puff pastry, thawed

2 tablespoons flaked almonds

METHOD

1. Cream together the butter and sugar, stir in the almond meal, apricots and almost all of the egg, keeping back a little for glazing.

2. Cut each sheet of puff pastry into 4 equal squares. Place on a lightly floured board; with a rolling pin, roll out to extend each side, making the square 13 x 13½cm to fit the recess.

3. Pre-heat the **Sandwich Maker**. Place a pastry square in each compartment, wider side to front. Spoon mixture into each triangular recess and cover with pastry top. Add a drop of milk to remaining egg and brush over pastry, sprinkle with flaked almonds. Close the lid and click the latch in place. Cook 5 minutes then release latch and cook 5 minutes more. The lid may lift as mixture swells.

4. Remove and trim excess pastry. Serve warm. Serve with ice cream.

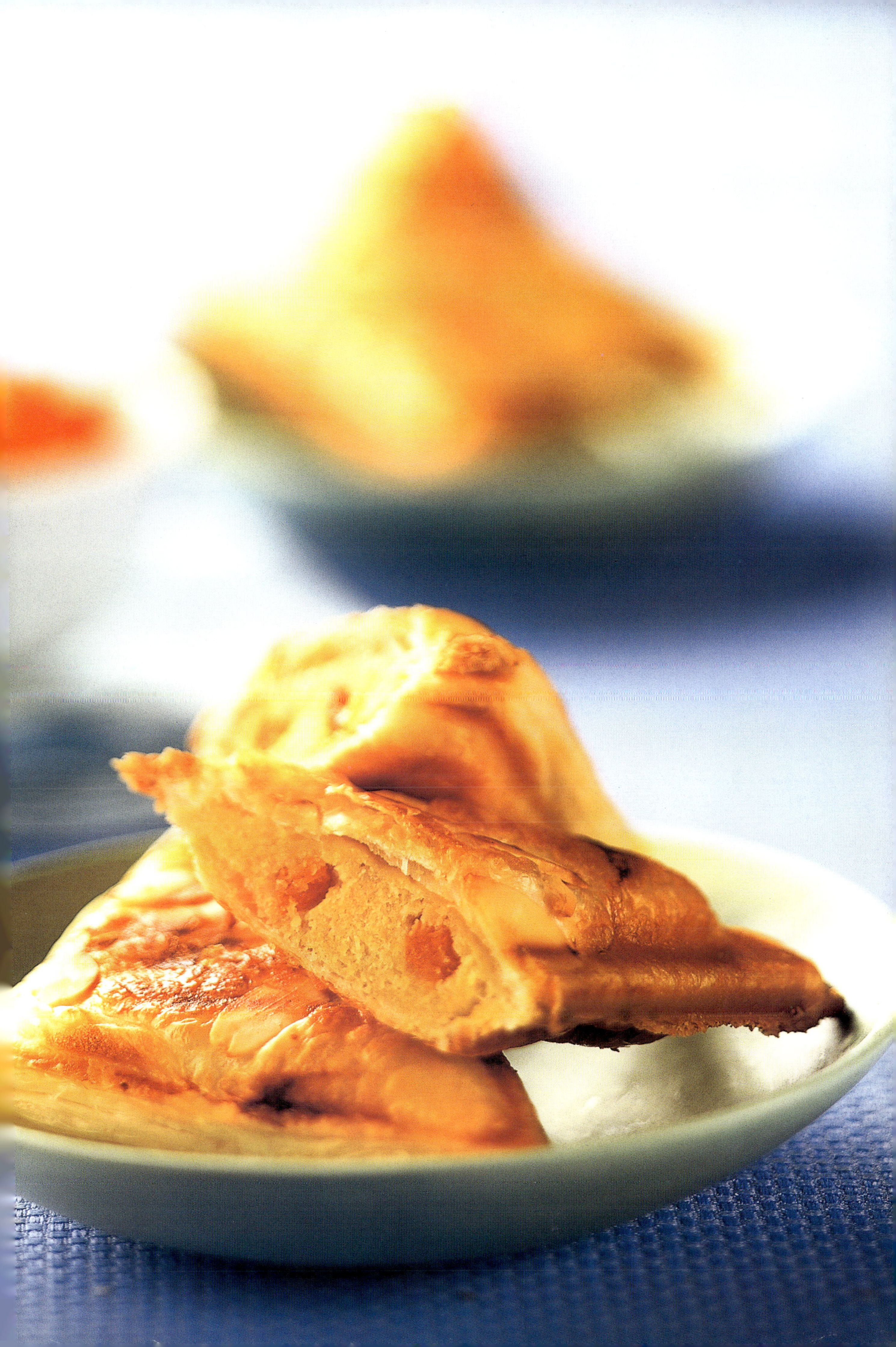

Flavoured spreads will add interest and variety in place of plain butter or margarine to spread

FLAVOURED SPREADS

o your toasted sandwiches. Use flavoured spreads
n the bread. Margarines may also be flavoured.

Method of Making

Bring the butter to room temperature. Place butter or margarine in a small bowl, add the flavouring ingredient and cream together with a wooden spoon. Use to spread on sandwich bread. Store remaining portion, covered in the refrigerator.

Chilli Butter

INGREDIENTS

60g butter

1 teaspoon MasterFoods Freshly Chopped Chilli

Tomato Mustard Butter

INGREDIENTS

60g butter

1½ teaspoons MasterFoods Tomato Mustard or MasterFoods American Style Mustard

Garlic Butter

INGREDIENTS

60g butter or margarine

¾ teaspoon MasterFoods Freshly Crushed Garlic

Pesto Butter

INGREDIENTS

60g butter

2 teaspoons MasterFoods Freshly Blended Basil

Garlic and Herb Butter

INGREDIENTS

60g butter

1 teaspoon MasterFoods Garlic Bread Seasoning

½ teaspoon MasterFoods Italian Herbs

Flavoured Mustard Butter

INGREDIENTS

60g butter

1½ teaspoons MasterFoods Honey Wholegrain Mustard or Masterfoods Seeded Honey Mustard

PRODUCTS AVAILABLE

With hundreds of products like mustards, marinades, sauces and spices, any cook can turn a simple meal into something special with MASTERFOODS.
Our entire range is full of flavour and easy to use, so even the busiest person can enjoy getting creative in the kitchen. And we've been arround for years, so you know you can rely on the quality. So try something quick and tasty from the MASTERFOODS range whenever you cook, then sit back and watch the complements roll in.

With MASTERFOODS sauces, mustards and herbs and spices, bringing authentic flavour to everything you cook is easy. Keep a range of our products in your fridge or pantry and you can bring life to even the simplest food in minutes, even the humble toasted sandwich.

Condiments

The MASTERFOODS range of condiments helps busy cooks give their meals extra flavour. Lift a simple steak with any of our mustards, from classic French and Australian styles to gourmet seeded or herb and tomato varieties. A MASTERFOODS pickle goes well with sandwiches, or you could even try a dollop of chutney. Virtually any meat is enhanced with MASTERFOODS relishes.

How MASTERFOODS product lift a toasty occasion

Give a garlicy toasted focaccia an extra dimension with MASTERFOODS Tomato and Chilli Pickle, or try a squeeze of American Mustard and some freshly ground black pepper on the ever-popular steak sandwich. You can even create Indian-style wraps with some naan bread, chicken and MASTERFOODS Mango Chutney. With hundreds of MASTERFOODS products to choose from, there's no stopping you getting creative in the kitchen.

Mustards & Sauces

Add a professional touch to your food with MASTERFOODS sauces. The Seafood sauce range partners perfectly with fresh oysters, fish and prawns, or go retro with our creamy seafood cocktail sauces.

If Asian is more to your liking, complement a stir fry with Sweet and Sour Sauce or whip up some fresh spring rolls with MASTERFOODS Sweet Chilli Sauce. And if you favour a traditional meal once in a while, there's no going past a good roast lamb with MASTERFOODS Mint Jelly. Whatever your preference, there's a MASTERFOODS sauce to match.

Adding flavour is easy with MASTERFOODS mustards and sauces in unique squeezy bottles. Even your kids can dispense sauce or mustard onto their food with no drips, no mess and no teaspoons to wash up afterwards. MASTERFOODS squeezy bottles are unbreakable, so they are ideal to pack for your next picnic, barbecue or camping trip. You can't even lose the lid. MASTERFOODS squeezy bottles close with a simple twist of the nozzle.

Herbs & Spices

With our incredible variety of herbs and spices, you can rely on MASTERFOODS for taste and texture in any meal. Keep our dry herbs and spices on hand in your cupboard and savour the summery taste of basil and oregano all year round. If you're a more adventurous cook, try MASTERFOODS exotic Piri Piri seasoning or whole Cinnamon Quills. There's even freshly minced Chilli, Garlic and Ginger to take the hassle out of adding authentic flavour to your cooking.

CHEESES AVAILABLE

Dairy Farmers offer the complete range of quality cheeses that give you the choice of flavour, texture and form to best suit your recipe. Use cheese on its own for a simple but comforting toasted cheese sandwich or combine cheeses to create your own signature dish! Select from Natural Cheddar Cheese, Specialty Cooking Cheese and Entertaining Cheese.

▼ COON Cheese was named after Edward William Coon, who, in 1926, patented a unique cheese making technique. Today Australians still enjoy eating COON cheese for its unique taste. Manufactured by Dairy Farmers, COON is proudly Australian made and owned.

Natural Cheddar Cheese

COON has that unique taste that Australians have known and loved for generations. Versatile natural cheddar, free from preservatives, COON is available in sliced, shredded and block format plus various flavours and fat contents. As well as the best-selling COON Tasty, other cheeses from COON include; Smooth & Mild - a softer creamier taste that kids prefer, and Extra Tasty - the unique COON taste with a little more bite. Lighter options consist of COON Light & Tasty, 25% less fat than regular cheddar, and COON Extra Light with 50% less fat.

Ideally suited to cooking applications, COON Natural Cheddars have excellent melting ability, providing good coverage for your pizza, tasty topping for melts and delicious fillings for toasted sandwiches, jaffles, and focaccia.

Cracker Barrel is a classic vintage cheddar with a distinctive sharpness. Available in Sharp, Extra Sharp and Special Reserve, Cracker Barrel can be a stand-alone cheese, served with crusty bread or crackers and is also at home on sandwiches.

Speciality Cooking Cheese

Mil Lel offers a range of authentic, specialty cooking cheeses including True Stretched Curd Pizza & Mozzarella, and Genuine Australian Grana Parmesan & Romano.

Excellent for cooking, Mil Lel Pizza and Mozzarella browns lightly, spreads evenly and stretches superbly. True 'stretched curd' cheeses have a soft mouth-feel and very little surface oil. Mil Lel Pizza cheese blends tasty cheddar with mozzarella for a unique pizza cheese flavour. Ideal for pizzas, Mil Lel Pizza and Mozzarella are great carriers for other flavours. Also try in pies, melts, and bakes.

Available in block and shredded formats, Mil Lel Parmesan and Romano are cut and shredded straight from wheels of Genuine Australian Grana cheese which are hand-turned, and aged to perfection. Vital in cooking, Mil Lel Parmesan and Romano adds robust flavour and appetite appeal to focaccia's, gourmet sandwiches, and pies.

▲ *Do you know... how to tell Genuine Grana cheese from imitations? Genuine Parmesan is one that the Italians call Grana. Hard, grainy-textured cheeses of unmistakable flavour and character made in the centuries-old Italian tradition, then hand turned and naturally aged to maturity. Many 'parmesans' are actually modified cheddars; young cheeses with an 'imitation' parmesan flavour.*
Mil Lel Parmesan & Romano are the genuine article, cut and shredded straight from wheels of Genuine Australian Grana Cheese.

Entertaining Cheese

Fred Walker offers a range of specialty entertaining cheeses including Waxed Blue Vein, Double Cream Camembert, Swiss, and Vintage Cheddar.

Equally at home on the cheese-platter or in cooking, the Fred Walker range is ideal for entertaining. Strong cheeses such as the Blue Vein are best combined with other robust ingredients that balance out its rich, spicy flavour; Blue Vein works well melted into sweet and savoury dishes. Milder cheeses such as Swiss add flavour and body to focaccia and sandwiches.

INDEX

APPLE CHARLOTTE	71
APRICOT AND ALMOND PUFFS	88
BACON AND EGG BUNS	14
BLUE VEIN CHEESE AND DATE TRIANGLES	83
BLUE VEIN RELISH	20
BREAD AND BUTTER CUSTARD	72
BRUSCHETTA	51
CARROT AND SULTANA	9
CHEESE TRIANGLES WITH FILO PASTRY	84
CHICKEN AND AVOCADO POCKET BREAD	13
CHICKEN AND GUACAMOLE	28
CHICKEN AND VEGETABLE PIE	65
CHICKEN SALAD AND CHEESE LAVASH ROLL	36
COCKTAIL SANDWICH	20
CORN, CHICKEN AND ASPARAGUS MELTS	26
ENTERTAINERS	80
ENTERTAINING IDEAS	51
FILLING COMBINATIONS	76
Apricot Chicken	76
Bacon and Pineapple	76
Prawn Cocktail	76
Prune, Walnut and Tasty Cheese	76
Ham, Swiss Cheese and Tomato	76
Baked Beans and Apple	77
Potato Mash Supreme	77
Salmon Salad	77
Sweet and Sour Chicken	79
Sausage Sizzle	79
FINGER FOOD MELTS	52
FLAVOURED SPREADS	91
Garlic Butter	91
Garlic and Herb Butter	91
Chilli Butter	91
Tomato Mustard Butter	91
Pesto Butter	91
Flavoured Mustard Butter	91
FRESH APPLE PIE	68
FRESH APPLE TRIANGLES	86
GOURMET SANDWICHES AND FOCACCIAS	28
GOURMET TOASTED SANDWICHES	10
GRILLED CAPSICUM AND ARTICHOKE PIZZA	23
GRILLED CHICKEN AND VEGETABLE FOCACCIA	42
HAM AND EGG PIE	62
HAM AND MUSHROOM MELTS	24
HERBED HAM PIE	66
HONEY, MUSTARD AND HAM	20
INTRODUCTION	**4**
ITALIAN STYLE FOCACCIA	40
JAFFLE MAKER RECIPES	**56**
JAFFLE SNACKS	56
MASTERFOODS AND COON PRODUCTS	92
MUFFIN BREAK	18
NACHO PLATTER	80
PEACH AND ALMOND TART	72
PEPPERONI TOMATO PIZZA	44
PESTO AND SEMI-DRIED TOMATO	20
PESTO CHEESE TRIANGLES	55
PIZZAS AND MELTS (SANDWICH PRESS)	44
PIZZAS AND MELTS (SANDWICH GRILL)	23
QUICK AND SIMPLE PIZZA	23
QUICK CHEESE CAKE	71
QUICK CUSTARD PIE	86
ROAST BEEF WITH HORSERADISH CREAM	48
ROAST LAMB AND VEGETABLES	59
ROAST PUMPKIN SNACK	56
SALMON AND CREAM CHEESE FOCACCIA	39
SALMON OR TUNA SNACK	58
SALMON PIE	66
SALMON WITH LEMON TARTARE	31
SANDWICH GRILL RECIPES	**8**
SANDWICH MAKER RECIPES	**74**
SANDWICH PRESS RECIPES	**28**
SAUSAGE SIZZLE ON SOURDOUGH	32
SAVOURY PLATTER	20
SAVOURY PLATTER TOPPINGS	20
SIMPLE TOASTED SANDWICHES	8
SIMPLE TOASTED SANDWICHES - FILLINGS	8
Ham and Cheese filling	8
Ham, Tomato and Cheese filling	8
Cheese and Chutney filling	8
Pizza Style	8
Parmesan Chicken	8
Cheese and Gherkin	8
Ham and Relish	8
Egg and Honey Mustard	8
Fruit Loaf and Cheese	9
SPINACH PIE	62
STEAK AND MUSHROOM STACK ON PIDE BUN	35
STEAK SANDWICH DELUXE	17
SWEET TREATS	87
SWEETS	68
TASTY AUSSIE PIE	61
TOMATO AND BASIL MELTS	47
TUNA AND MUSHROOM PIZZA	47
TURKEY AND CRANBERRY BAGELS	39
TURKEY AND GRILLED ORANGE WITH FENNEL ON PIDE	43
TURKEY AND RELISH	20
TYPES OF SNACKMAKERS	6
VEGETABLE AND CHEESE SANDWICH	10